MW00989046

PRAYER BOOK

Holy Trinity Monastery
Jordanville, N.Y.

Printed with the blessing
of the Holy Synod of Bishops
of the Russian Orthodox Church
Outside of Russia

Prayer Book © 2003 Holy Trinity Monastery

PRINTSHOP OF
SAINT JOB OF POCHAEV

An imprint of

HOLY TRINITY PUBLICATIONS
Holy Trinity Monastery
Jordanville, New York 13361-0036
www.holytrinitypublications.com

ISBN 978-088465-175-8

Fourth Edition — Revised 2005
Reprinting—2024

CONTENTS

MORNING PRAYERS

Having risen from sleep, before any other action, stand reverently, considering thyself to be in the presence of the All-seeing God, and, having made the sign of the Cross, say:

In the name of the Father, and of the Son, and of the Holy Spirit. Amen.

Then pause a moment, until all thy senses are calmed and thy thoughts forsake all things earthly; and then make three bows, saying:

The Prayer of the Publican:

O God, be merciful to me a sinner.

The Beginning Prayer:

O Lord Jesus Christ, Son of God, for the sake of the prayers of Thy most pure Mother and all the saints, have mercy on us. Amen.

Glory to Thee, our God, glory to Thee.

O Heavenly King, Comforter, Spirit of Truth, Who art everywhere present and fillest all things, Treasury of good things and Giver of life: Come and dwell in us, and cleanse us of all impurity, and save our souls, O Good One.

Holy God, Holy Mighty, Holy Immortal, have mercy on us. *Thrice.*

Glory to the Father, and to the Son, and to the Holy Spirit, both now and ever, and unto the ages of ages. Amen.

O Most Holy Trinity, have mercy on us. O Lord, blot out our sins. O Master, pardon our iniquities. O Holy One, visit and heal our infirmities for Thy name's sake.

Lord, have mercy. *Thrice.*

Glory to the Father, and to the Son,

and to the Holy Spirit, both now and
ever, and unto the ages of ages. Amen.

Our Father, Who art in the heavens,
hallowed be Thy name. Thy kingdom
come, Thy will be done, on earth as it
is in heaven. Give us this day our daily
bread, and forgive us our debts, as we
forgive our debtors; and lead us not
into temptation, but deliver us from
the evil one.

Troparia to the Holy Trinity:

Having risen from sleep, we fall
down before Thee, O Good One, and
the angelical hymn we cry aloud to
Thee, O Mighty One: Holy, Holy, Holy
art Thou, O God; through the
Theotokos, have mercy on us.

Glory to the Father, and to the Son,
and to the Holy Spirit.

From bed and sleep hast Thou raised
me up, O Lord: enlighten my mind
and heart, and open my lips that I may

hymn Thee, O Holy Trinity: Holy, Holy, Holy art Thou, O God; through the Theotokos, have mercy on us.

Both now and ever, and unto the ages of ages. Amen.

Suddenly the Judge shall come, and the deeds of each shall be laid bare; but with fear do we cry at midnight: Holy, Holy, Holy art Thou, O God; through the Theotokos, have mercy on us.

Lord, have mercy. *Twelve.*

Prayer of Saint Basil the Great to the Most Holy Trinity:

As I rise from sleep, I thank Thee, O Holy Trinity, for through Thy great goodness and patience Thou wast not angry with me, an idler and sinner, nor hast Thou destroyed me with mine iniquities, but hast shown Thy usual love for mankind; and when I was prostrate in despair, Thou hast raised me up to keep the morning watch and glorify Thy power. And now enlighten my mind's eye, and open my mouth that I may meditate on Thy words, and understand Thy commandments, and do Thy will, and hymn Thee in heartfelt confession, and sing praises to Thine all-holy name: of the Father, and of the Son, and of the Holy Spirit, now and ever, and unto the ages of ages. Amen.

O come let us worship God our King.

O come let us worship and fall down before Christ our King and God.

O come let us worship and fall down before Christ Himself, our King and God.

PSALM 50

Have mercy on me, O God, according to Thy great mercy; and according to the multitude of Thy compassions blot out my transgression. Wash me thoroughly from mine iniquity, and cleanse me from my sin. For I know mine iniquity, and my sin is ever before me. Against Thee only have I sinned and done this evil before Thee, that Thou mightest be justified in Thy words, and prevail when Thou art judged. For behold, I was conceived in iniquities, and in sins did my mother bear me. For behold, Thou hast loved truth; the hidden and secret things of Thy wisdom hast Thou made manifest unto me. Thou shalt sprinkle me with hyssop, and I shall be made clean; Thou shalt wash me, and I shall be made whiter than snow. Thou shalt make me to hear joy and gladness; the bones that be humbled, they shall rejoice. Turn Thy face away from my sins, and blot out all mine iniquities. Create in me a clean heart, O God,

and renew a right spirit within me.
Cast me not away from Thy presence,
and take not Thy Holy Spirit from me.
Restore unto me the joy of Thy salvation, and with Thy governing Spirit
establish me. I shall teach transgressors Thy ways, and the ungodly shall
turn back unto Thee. Deliver me from
blood-guiltiness, O God, Thou God of
my salvation; my tongue shall rejoice
in Thy righteousness. O Lord, Thou
shalt open my lips, and my mouth shall
declare Thy praise. For if Thou hadst
desired sacrifice, I had given it; with
whole-burnt offerings Thou shalt not
be pleased. A sacrifice unto God is a
broken spirit; a heart that is broken
and humbled God will not despise. Do
good, O Lord, in Thy good pleasure
unto Sion, and let the walls of
Jerusalem be builded. Then shalt
Thou be pleased with a sacrifice of

righteousness, with oblation and whole-burnt offerings. Then shall they offer bullocks upon Thine altar.

The Symbol of the Orthodox Faith:

I believe in one God, the Father Almighty, Maker of heaven and earth, and of all things visible and invisible. And in one Lord Jesus Christ, the Son of God, the Only-begotten, begotten of the Father before all ages; Light of Light; true God of true God; begotten, not made; of one essence with the Father; by Whom all things were made; Who for us men, and for our salvation, came down from the heavens, and was incarnate of the Holy Spirit and the Virgin Mary, and became man; And was crucified for us under Pontius Pilate, and suffered, and was buried; And arose again on the third day according to the Scriptures; And ascended into the heavens, and sitteth at the right hand of the Father; And shall come again, with glory, to judge both the living and the dead; Whose kingdom shall have no end. And in the Holy Spirit, the Lord, the Giver of Life; Who proceedeth from the Father; Who with the Father and the Son together is worshipped and glorified; Who spake by the prophets. In One, Holy, Catholic, and Apostolic Church. I confess one baptism for the remission of sins. I look for the resurrection of the dead, And the life of the age to come. Amen.

Prayer I, of St. Macarius the Great:

O God, cleanse me a sinner, for I have never done anything good in Thy sight; but deliver me from the evil one, and let Thy will be done in me, that I may open mine unworthy mouth without condemnation, and praise Thy holy name: of the Father, and of the Son, and of the Holy Spirit, now and ever, and unto the ages of ages. Amen.

Prayer II, of the same saint:

Having risen from sleep, I offer unto Thee, O Saviour, the midnight hymn, and falling down I cry unto Thee: Grant me not to fall asleep in the death of sin, but have compassion on me, O Thou Who wast voluntarily crucified, and hasten to raise me who am reclining in idleness, and save me in prayer and intercession; and after the night's sleep shine upon me a sinless day, O Christ God, and save me.

Prayer III, of the same saint:

Having risen from sleep, I hasten to Thee, O Master, Lover of mankind, and by Thy loving-kindness, I strive to do Thy work, and I pray to

Thee: Help me at all times, in every-thing, and deliver me from every worldly, evil thing and every impulse of the devil, and save me, and lead me into Thine eternal kingdom. For Thou art my Creator, and the Giver and Provider of everything good, and in Thee is all my hope, and unto Thee do I send up glory, now and ever, and unto the ages of ages. Amen.

Prayer IV, of the same saint:

O Lord, Who in Thine abundant goodness and Thy great compas-sion hast granted me, Thy servant, to go through the time of the night that is past without attack from any opposing evil: Do Thou Thyself, O Master, Creator of all things, vouchsafe me by Thy true light and with an enlightened heart to do Thy will, now and ever, and unto the ages of ages. Amen.

Prayer V, of St. Basil the Great:

O Lord Almighty, God of hosts and of all flesh, Who dwellest on high and lookest down on things that are lowly, Who searchest the heart and innermost being, and clearly fore-knowest the secrets of men; O unoriginate and everlasting Light, with Whom is no variableness, neither shadow of turning: Do Thou, O Immortal King, receive our supplications which we, daring because of the multitude of Thy compassions, offer Thee at the present time from defiled lips; and forgive us our sins, in deed, word, and thought, whether committed by us knowingly or in ignorance, and cleanse us from every defilement of flesh and spirit. And grant us to pass through the night of the whole present life with watchful heart and sober thought, ever expecting the coming of the bright and appointed day of Thine Only-begotten Son, our Lord and God and Saviour, Jesus Christ, whereon the Judge of all shall come with glory to reward each according to his deeds. May we not be found fallen and idle, but watching, and upright in activity, ready to accompany Him into the joy and divine palace of His glory, where there is the ceaseless sound of those that keep festival, and the unspeakable delight of those that behold the ineffable beauty of Thy countenance. For Thou art the true Light that enlightenest and sanctifiest all, and all creation doth hymn Thee unto the ages of ages. Amen.

Prayer VI, likewise by St. Basil:

We bless Thee, O Most High God and Lord of mercy, Who ever doest with us things both great and inscrutable, both glorious and awe-some, of which there is no measure; Who grantest to us sleep for rest from our infirmities, and relaxation from the labours of our much-toiling flesh. We thank Thee that Thou hast not destroyed us with our iniquities, but hast shown Thy loving-kindness to man as usual, and while we were lying in despair upon our beds, Thou hast raised us up that we might glorify Thy dominion. Wherefore, we implore Thy boundless goodness: Enlighten the eyes of our understanding and raise up our mind from the heavy sleep of indolence; open our mouth and fill it with Thy praise, that we may be able steadily to hymn and confess Thee, Who art God glorified in all and by all, the unoriginate Father, with Thine Only-begotten Son, and Thine All-holy and good and life-creating

Spirit, now and ever, and unto the ages of ages. Amen.

Prayer VII,
to the Most Holy Theotokos:

I sing of thy grace, O Sovereign Lady, and I pray thee to grace my mind. Teach me to step aright in the way of Christ's commandments. Strengthen me to keep awake in song, and drive away the sleep of despondency. O Bride of God, by thy prayers release me, bound with the bonds of sin. Guard me by night and by day, and deliver me from foes that defeat me. O bearer of God the Life-giver, enliven me who am deadened by passions. O bearer of the Unwaning Light, enlighten my blinded soul. O marvellous palace of the Master, make me to be a house of the Divine Spirit. O bearer of the Healer, heal the perennial passions of my soul. Guide me to

the path of repentance, for I am tossed
in the storm of life. Deliver me from
eternal fire, and from evil worms, and
from Tartarus. Let me not be exposed
to the rejoicing of demons, guilty as I
am of many sins. Renew me, grown
old from senseless sins, O most immaculate one. Present me untouched by
all torments, and pray for me to the
Master of all. Vouchsafe me to find the
joys of heaven with all the saints. O
most holy Virgin, hearken unto the
voice of thine unprofitable servant.
Grant me torrents of tears, O most
pure one, to cleanse my soul from
impurity. I offer the groans of my
heart to thee unceasingly, strive for
me, O Sovereign Lady. Accept my service of supplication and offer it to compassionate God. O thou who art above
the angels, raise me above this world's
confusion. O Light-bearing heavenly

tabernacle, direct the grace of the Spirit in me. I raise my hands and lips in thy praise, defiled as they are by impurity, O all-immaculate one. Deliver me from soul-corrupting evils, and fervently intercede with Christ, to Whom is due honour and worship, now and ever, and unto the ages of ages. Amen.

Prayer VIII,
to our Lord Jesus Christ:

O my plenteously-merciful and all-merciful God, Lord Jesus Christ, through Thy great love Thou didst come down and become incarnate so that Thou mightest save all. And again, O Saviour, save me by Thy grace, I pray Thee. For if Thou shouldst save me for my works, this would not be grace or a gift, but rather a duty; yea, Thou Who art great in compassion and ineffable in mercy. For he that believeth in Me,

Thou hast said, O my Christ, shall live
and never see death. If, then, faith in
Thee saveth the desperate, behold, I
believe, save me, for Thou art my
God and Creator. Let faith instead of
works be imputed to me, O my God,
for Thou wilt find no works which
could justify me. But may my faith suf-
fice instead of all works, may it answer
for, may it acquit me, may it make me
a partaker of Thine eternal glory. And
let Satan not seize me and boast,
O Word, that he hath torn me from
Thy hand and fold. But whether I
desire it or not, save me, O Christ my
Saviour, forestall me quickly, quickly,
for I perish. Thou art my God from my
mother's womb. Vouchsafe me,
O Lord, to love Thee now as fervently
as I once loved sin itself, and also to
work for Thee without idleness,
diligently, as I worked before for

deceptive Satan. But supremely shall I work for Thee, my Lord and God, Jesus Christ, all the days of my life, now and ever, and unto the ages of ages. Amen.

Prayer IX,
to the Holy Guardian Angel:

O holy angel that standeth by my wretched soul and my passionate life, forsake not me a sinner, nor shrink from me because of mine intemperance. Give no place for the cunning demon to master me through the violence of my mortal body, strengthen my poor and feeble hand, and guide me in the way of salvation. Yea, O holy angel of God, guardian and protector of my wretched soul and body, forgive me all wherein I have offended thee all the days of my life; and if I have sinned during the past night, protect me during the present day, and guard me from every temptation of the enemy, that I may not anger God by any sin. And pray to the Lord for me, that He may establish me in His fear, and show me, His servant, to be worthy of His goodness. Amen.

Prayer X, to the Most Holy Theotokos:

O my most holy lady Theotokos, through thy holy and all-powerful prayers, banish from me, thy lowly and wretched servant, despondency, forgetfulness, folly, carelessness, and all filthy, evil, and blasphemous thoughts from my wretched heart and my darkened mind. And quench the flame of my passions, for I am poor and wretched, and deliver me from many and cruel memories and deeds, and free me from all their evil effects. For blessed art thou by all generations, and glorified is thy most honourable name unto the ages of ages. Amen.

Prayer for the Salvation of the Nation:

O Lord Jesus Christ our God, forgive our iniquities. Through the intercessions of Thy most pure Mother, grant our rulers peaceful governance so that in their calm we may also live in all godliness and modesty. Amen.

Prayerful Invocation of the Saint Whose Name we bear:

Pray unto God for me, O holy Godpleaser *N.*, for I fervently flee unto Thee, the speedy helper and intercessor for my soul.

Song to the Most Holy Theotokos:

O Theotokos and Virgin, rejoice, Mary, full of grace, the Lord is with thee; blessed art thou among women, and blessed is the Fruit of thy womb, for thou hast borne the Saviour of our souls.

Troparion to the Cross:

Save, O Lord, Thy people, and bless Thine inheritance; grant Thou victory to Orthodox Christians over enemies; and by the power of Thy Cross do Thou preserve Thy commonwealth.

Then offer a brief prayer for the health and salvation of thy spiritual father, thy parents, relatives, those in authority, benefactors, others known to thee, the ailing, or those passing through sorrows.

And if it be possible, read this commemoration:

For the Living:

Remember, O Lord Jesus Christ our God, Thy mercies and compassions which are from the ages, for the sake of which Thou didst become man and didst will to endure crucifixion and death for the salvation of those that rightly believe in Thee; and having risen from the dead didst ascend into the heavens and sittest at the right hand of God the Father, and regardest the humble entreaties of those that call upon Thee with all their heart; incline Thine ear, and hearken unto the humble supplication of me, Thine unprofitable servant, as an odor of spiritual fragrance, which I offer unto Thee for all Thy people. And first, remember Thy Holy, Catholic, and Apostolic Church, which Thou hast provided through Thine honourable Blood, and establish, and strengthen, and expand, increase, pacify, and keep Her unconquerable by the gates of hades; calm the dissensions of the churches, quench the raging of the nations, and quickly destroy and uproot the rising of heresy, and bring them to nought by the power of Thy Holy Spirit. *Bow.*

Save, O Lord, and have mercy on the Russian Land and her Orthodox people both in the homeland and in the diaspora, this land and its authorities. *Bow.*

Save, O Lord, and have mercy on the holy Eastern Orthodox patriarchs, most reverend metropolitans, Orthodox archbishops and bishops, and all the priestly and monastic order, and all who serve in the Church, whom Thou hast appointed to shepherd Thy rational flock, and through their prayers have mercy and save me, a sinner. *Bow.*

Save, O Lord, and have mercy on my spiritual father *N.*, and through his holy prayers forgive my sins. *Bow.*

Save, O Lord, and have mercy on my parents, *Names,* brothers and sisters, and my kindred according to the flesh, and all the neighbours of my family and friends, and grant them

Thine earthly and spiritual good things. *Bow.*

Save, O Lord, and have mercy on the aged and the young, the poor and the orphans and widows, and those in sickness and sorrow, misfortune and tribulation, those in difficult circumstances and in captivity, in prisons and dungeons, and especially those of Thy servants that are persecuted for Thy sake and the Orthodox Faith by godless peoples, by apostates, and by heretics; and remember them, visit, strengthen, comfort, and by Thy power quickly grant them relief, freedom, and deliverance. *Bow.*

Save, O Lord, and have mercy on them that hate and wrong me, and make temptation for me, and let them not perish because of me, a sinner. *Bow.*

Illumine with the light of awareness

the apostates from the Orthodox Faith, and those blinded by pernicious heresies, and number them with Thy Holy, Apostolic, Catholic Church. *Bow.*

For the Departed:

Remember, O Lord, those that have departed this life, Orthodox kings and queens, princes and princesses, most holy patriarchs, most reverend metropolitans, Orthodox archbishops and bishops, those in priestly and clerical orders of the Church, and those that have served Thee in the monastic order, and grant them rest with the saints in Thine eternal tabernacles. *Bow.*

Remember, O Lord, the souls of Thy departed servants, my parents, *Names,* and all my kindred according to the flesh; and forgive them all transgressions, voluntary and involuntary, granting them the kingdom and a portion of Thine eternal good things, and the delight of Thine endless and blessed life. *Bow.*

Remember, O Lord, also all our fathers and brethren, and sisters, and those that lie here, and all Orthodox Christians that departed in the hope of resurrection and life eternal, and settle them with Thy saints, where the light of Thy countenance shall visit them, and have mercy on us, for Thou art good and the Lover of mankind. *Bow.*

Grant, O Lord, remission of sins to all our fathers, brethren, and sisters that have departed before us in the faith and hope of resurrection, and make their memory to be eternal. *Bow.*

Final Prayer:

It is truly meet to bless thee, the Theotokos, ever-blessed and most blameless, and Mother of our God.

More honourable than the Cherubim, and beyond compare more glorious than the Seraphim, who without corruption gavest birth to God the Word, the very Theotokos, thee do we magnify.

Glory to the Father, and to the Son, and to the Holy Spirit, both now and ever, and unto the ages of ages. Amen.

Lord, have mercy. *Thrice.*

O Lord, bless. *And the dismissal:*

O Lord Jesus Christ, Son of God, for the sake of the prayers of Thy most pure Mother, our holy and God-bearing fathers and all the saints, have mercy on us. Amen.

PRAYERS DURING THE DAY

Before the Beginning of Any Work:

O Lord, bless. *Or:*

O Lord Jesus Christ, Only-begotten Son of Thine unoriginate Father, Thou hast said with Thy most pure lips: For without Me, ye can do nothing. My Lord, O Lord, in faith having embraced Thy words, I fall down before Thy goodness; help me, a sinner, to complete through Thee Thyself this work which I am about to begin, in the name of the Father, and of the Son, and of the Holy Spirit. Amen.

After the Completion of Any Work:

Glory to Thee, O Lord. *Or:*

Thou art the fullness of all good things, O my Christ; fill my soul with joy and gladness, and save me, for Thou alone art plenteous in mercy.

Before Lessons:

O Heavenly King, Comforter, Spirit of Truth, Who art everywhere present and fillest all things, Treasury of good things and Giver of life: Come and dwell in us, and cleanse us of all impurity, and save our souls, O Good One.

Or:

O Most-good Lord! Send down upon us the grace of Thy Holy Spirit, Who granteth gifts and strengtheneth the powers of our souls, so that by attending to the teaching given us, we may grow to the glory of Thee, our Creator, to the comfort of our parents, and to the service of the Church and our native land.

After Lessons:

It is truly meet to bless thee, the Theotokos, ever-blessed and most blameless and Mother of our God. More honourable than the Cherubim, and beyond compare more glorious than the Seraphim; who without corruption gavest birth to God the Word, the very Theotokos, thee do we magnify.

Or:

We thank Thee, O Creator, that Thou hast vouchsafed us Thy grace to attend instruction. Bless our leaders, parents, and instructors who are leading us to an awareness of good, and grant us power and strength to continue this study.

**Before [Breakfast and] Noon
and Evening Meals:**

Our Father, Who art in the heavens, hallowed be Thy name. Thy kingdom come, Thy will be done, on earth as it is in heaven. Give us this day our daily bread, and forgive us our debts, as we forgive our debtors; and lead us not into temptation, but deliver us from the evil one.

Or:

The eyes of all look to Thee with hope, and Thou gavest them their food in due season. Thou openest Thy hand and fillest every living thing with Thy favour.

After [Breakfast and] Noon and Evening Meals:

We thank Thee, O Christ our God, that Thou hast satisfied us with Thine earthly gifts; deprive us not of Thy heavenly kingdom, but as Thou camest among Thy disciples, O Saviour, and gavest them peace, come to us and save us.

PRAYERS BEFORE SLEEP

In the name of the Father, and of the Son, and of the Holy Spirit. Amen.

O Lord Jesus Christ, Son of God, for the sake of the prayers of Thy most pure Mother, of our holy and God-bearing fathers and all the saints, have mercy on us. Amen.

Glory to Thee, our God, glory to Thee.

O Heavenly King, Comforter, Spirit of Truth, Who art everywhere present and fillest all things, Treasury of good things and Giver of life: Come and dwell in us, and cleanse us of all impurity, and save our souls, O Good One.

Holy God, Holy Mighty, Holy Immortal, have mercy on us. *Thrice.*

Glory to the Father, and to the Son, and to the Holy Spirit, both now and ever, and unto the ages of ages. Amen.

O Most Holy Trinity, have mercy on us. O Lord, blot out our sins. O Master, pardon our iniquities. O Holy One, visit and heal our infirmities for Thy name's sake.

Lord, have mercy. *Thrice.*

Glory to the Father, and to the Son, and to the Holy Spirit, both now and ever, and unto the ages of ages. Amen.

Our Father, Who art in the heavens, hallowed be Thy name. Thy kingdom come, Thy will be done, on earth as it is in heaven. Give us this day our daily bread, and forgive us our debts, as we forgive our debtors; and lead us not into temptation, but deliver us from the evil one.

Troparia:

Have mercy on us, O Lord, have

mercy on us; for at a loss for any defence, this prayer do we sinners offer unto Thee as Master: have mercy on us.

Glory to the Father, and to the Son, and to the Holy Spirit.

Lord, have mercy on us; for we have hoped in Thee, be not angry with us greatly, neither remember our iniquities; but look upon us now as Thou art compassionate, and deliver us from our enemies, for Thou art our God, and we, Thy people; all are the works of the Thy hands, and we call upon Thy name.

Both now and ever, and unto the ages of ages. Amen.

The door of compassion open unto us, O blessed Theotokos, for, hoping in thee, let us not perish; through thee may we be delivered from adversities, for thou art the salvation of the

Christian race.

Lord, have mercy. *Twelve times.*

Prayer I, of St. Macarius the Great:

O Eternal God and King of all creation, Who hast vouchsafed me to
arrive at this hour, forgive me the sins
that I have committed this day in deed,
word, and thought; and cleanse, O
Lord, my lowly soul of all impurity of
flesh and spirit, and grant me, O Lord,
to pass the sleep of this night in peace;
that, rising from my lowly bed, I may
please Thy most holy name all the days
of my life, and thwart the enemies,
fleshly and bodiless, that war against
me. And deliver me, O Lord, from vain
thoughts and evil desires which defile
me. For Thine is the kingdom, and
the power, and the glory: of the Father,
and of the Son, and of the Holy Spirit,
now and ever, and unto the ages of
ages. Amen.

Prayer II, of Saint Antiochus:

O Ruler of all, Word of the Father, O Jesus Christ, Thou Who art perfect: For the sake of the plenitude of Thy mercy, never depart from me, but always remain in me Thy servant. O Jesus, Good Shepherd of Thy sheep, deliver me not over to the sedition of the serpent, and leave me not to the will of Satan, for the seed of corruption is in me. But do Thou, O Lord, worshipful God, holy King, Jesus Christ, as I sleep, guard me by the Unwaning Light, Thy Holy Spirit, by Whom Thou didst sanctify Thy disciples. O Lord, grant me, Thine unworthy servant, Thy salvation upon my bed. Enlighten my mind with the light of understanding of Thy Holy Gospel; my soul, with the love of Thy Cross; my heart, with the purity of Thy word; my body, with Thy passionless Passion.

Keep my thought in Thy humility, and raise me up at the proper time for Thy glorification. For most glorified art Thou together with Thine unoriginate Father, and the Most-holy Spirit, unto the ages. Amen.

Prayer III, to the Holy Spirit:

O Lord, Heavenly King, Comforter, Spirit of Truth, show compassion and have mercy on me Thy sinful servant, and loose me from mine unworthiness, and forgive all wherein I have sinned against Thee today as a man, and not only as a man, but even worse than a beast, my sins voluntary and involuntary, known and unknown, whether from youth, and from evil suggestion, or whether from brazenness and despondency. If I have sworn by Thy name, or blasphemed it in my thought; or reproached anyone, or slandered anyone in mine anger, or

grieved anyone, or have become angry
about anything; or have lied, or slept
needlessly, or if a beggar hath come to
me and I disdained him; or if I have
grieved my brother, or have quarreled,
or have condemned anyone; or if I
have been boastful, or prideful, or
angry; if, as I stood at prayer, my mind
hath been distracted by the wiles of
this world, or by thoughts of depravity;
if I have over-eaten, or have drunk
excessively, or laughed frivolously; if I
have thought evil, or seen the beauty
of another and been wounded thereby
in my heart; if I have said improper
things, or derided my brother's sin
when mine own sins are countless; if I
have been neglectful of prayer, or have
done some other wrong that I do not
remember, for all of this and more
than this have I done: have mercy, O
Master my Creator, on me Thy down-

cast and unworthy servant, and loose
me, and remit, and forgive me, for
Thou art good and the Lover of
mankind, so that, lustful, sinful, and
wretched as I am, I may lie down and
sleep and rest in peace. And I shall
worship, and hymn, and glorify Thy
most honourable name, together with
the Father and His Only-begotten Son,
now and ever, and unto the ages. Amen.

Prayer IV, of St. Macarius the Great:

What shall I offer Thee, or what
shall I give Thee, O greatly-gifted,
immortal King, O compassionate Lord
Who lovest mankind? For though I
have been slothful in pleasing Thee,
and have done nothing good, Thou
hast led me to the close of this day that
is past, establishing the conversion and
salvation of my soul. Be merciful to me
a sinner, bereft of every good deed,
raise up my fallen soul which hath

become defiled by countless sins, and
take away from me every evil thought
of this visible life. Forgive my sins, O
Only Sinless One, in which I have
sinned against Thee this day, known or
unknown, in word, and deed, and
thought, and in all my senses. Do
Thou Thyself protect and guard me
from every opposing circumstance, by
Thy Divine authority and power and
inexpressible love for mankind. Blot
out, O God, blot out the multitude of
my sins. Be pleased, O Lord, to deliver me from the net of the evil one, and
save my passionate soul, and overshad-
ow me with the light of Thy countenance when Thou shalt come in glory;
and cause me, uncondemned now, to
sleep a dreamless sleep, and keep Thy
servant untroubled by thoughts, and
drive away from me all satanic deeds;
and enlighten for me the eyes of my

heart with understanding, lest I sleep unto death. And send me an angel of peace, a guardian and guide of my soul and body, that he may deliver me from mine enemies; that, rising from my bed, I may offer Thee prayers of thanksgiving. Yea, O Lord, hearken unto me, Thy sinful and wretched servant, in confession and conscience; grant me, when I arise, to be instructed by Thy sayings; and through Thine angels cause demonic despondency to be driven far from me: that I may bless Thy holy name, and glorify and extol the most pure Theotokos Mary, whom Thou hast given to us sinners as a protectress, and accept her who prayeth for us. For I know that she exemplifieth Thy love for mankind and prayeth for us without ceasing. Through her protection, and the sign of the precious Cross, and for the sake of all Thy saints, preserve my wretched soul, O Jesus Christ our God: for holy art Thou, and most glorious for ever. Amen.

Prayer V:

O Lord our God, as Thou art good and the Lover of mankind, forgive me wherein I have sinned today in word, deed, and thought. Grant me peaceful and undisturbed sleep; send Thy guardian angel to protect and keep me from all evil. For Thou art the Guardian of our souls and bodies, and unto Thee do we send up glory: to the Father, and to the Son, and to the Holy Spirit, now and ever, and unto the ages of ages. Amen.

Prayer VI:

O Lord our God, in Whom we believe and Whose name we invoke above every name, grant us, as we go to sleep, relaxation of soul and body, and keep us from all dreams, and dark pleasures; stop the onslaught of the passions and quench the burnings that arise in the flesh. Grant us to live chastely in deed and word, that we may obtain a virtuous life, and not fall away from Thy promised blessings; for blessed art Thou for ever. Amen.

Prayer VII, of St. John Chrysostom, according to the number of hours of day and night:

O Lord, deprive me not of Thy heavenly good things. O Lord, deliver me from the eternal torments. O Lord, if I have sinned in mind or thought, in word or deed, forgive me. O Lord, deliver me from all ignorance, forgetfulness, faintheartedness, and stony insensibility. O Lord, deliver me from every temptation. O Lord, enlighten my heart which evil desire hath darkened. O Lord, as a man I have sinned, but do Thou, as the compassionate God, have mercy on me, seeing the infirmity of my soul. O Lord, send Thy grace to my help, that I may glorify Thy holy name. O Lord Jesus Christ, write me Thy servant in the Book of Life, and grant me a good end. O Lord my God, even though I have done nothing good in Thy sight, yet grant me by Thy grace to make a good beginning. O Lord, sprinkle into my heart the dew of Thy grace. O Lord of heaven and earth, remember me Thy sinful servant, shameful and unclean, in Thy kingdom. Amen.

O Lord, accept me in penitence. O Lord, forsake me not. O Lord, lead me not into temptation. O Lord, grant me good thoughts. O Lord, grant me tears, and remembrance of death, and compunction. O Lord, grant me the thought of confessing my sins.

O Lord, grant me humility, chastity, and obedience. O Lord, grant me patience, courage, and meekness. O Lord, implant in me the root of good, Thy fear in my heart. O Lord, vouchsafe me to love Thee with all my soul and thoughts, and in all things to do Thy will. O Lord, protect me from evil men, and demons, and passions, and from every other unseemly thing. O Lord, Thou knowest that Thou doest as Thou wilt: Thy will be done also in me a sinner; for blessed art Thou unto the ages. Amen.

Prayer VIII,
to our Lord Jesus Christ:

O Lord Jesus Christ, Son of God, for the sake of Thy most honourable Mother, and Thy bodiless angels, Thy Prophet and Forerunner and Baptist, the God-inspired apostles, the radiant and victorious martyrs, the holy and God-bearing fathers, and through the intercessions of all the saints, deliver me from the besetting presence of the demons. Yea, my Lord and Creator, Who desirest not the death of a sinner, but rather that he be converted and live, grant conversion also to me, wretched and unworthy; rescue me from the mouth of the pernicious serpent, who is yawning to devour me and take me down to hades alive. Yea, my Lord, my Comfort, Who for my miserable sake wast clothed in corruptible flesh, draw me out of misery, and grant comfort to my miserable soul. Implant in my heart to fulfill Thy commandments, and to forsake evil deeds, and to obtain Thy blessings; for in Thee, O Lord, have I hoped, save me.

Prayer IX,
to the Most Holy Theotokos:

O good Mother of the Good King, most pure and blessed Theotokos Mary, do thou pour out the mercy of thy Son and our God upon my passionate soul, and by thine intercessions guide me unto good works, that I may pass the remaining time of my life without blemish, and attain paradise through thee, O Virgin Theotokos, who alone art pure and blessed.

Prayer X, to the Holy Guardian Angel:

O Angel of Christ, my holy guardian and protector of my soul and body, forgive me all wherein I have sinned this day, and deliver me from all opposing evil of mine enemy, lest I anger my God by any sin. Pray for me, a sinful and unworthy servant, that thou mayest show me forth worthy of the kindness and mercy of the All-holy

Trinity, and of the Mother of my Lord
Jesus Christ, and of all the saints. Amen.
Kontakion to the Theotokos:

To thee, the Champion Leader, we
thy servants dedicate a feast of victory
and of thanksgiving as ones rescued
out of sufferings, O Theotokos; but as
thou art one with might which is invincible, from all dangers that can be do
thou deliver us, that we may cry to
thee: Rejoice, thou Bride Unwedded!

Most glorious, Ever-Virgin, Mother
of Christ God, present our prayer to
thy Son and our God, that through
thee He may save our souls.

All my hope I place in thee, O
Mother of God: keep me under thy
protection.

O Virgin Theotokos, disdain not me
a sinner, needing thy help and thy protection, and have mercy on me, for my
soul hath hoped in thee.

My hope is the Father, my refuge is the Son, my protection is the Holy Spirit: O Holy Trinity, glory to Thee.

It is truly meet to bless thee, the Theotokos, ever-blessed and most blameless, and Mother of our God. More honourable than the Cherubim, and beyond compare more glorious than the Seraphim, who without corruption gavest birth to God the Word, the very Theotokos, thee do we magnify.

Glory to the Father, and to the Son, and to the Holy Spirit, both now and ever, and unto the ages of ages. Amen.

Lord, have mercy. *Thrice.*

O Lord, bless. *And the dismissal:*

O Lord Jesus Christ, Son of God, for the sake of the prayers of Thy most pure Mother, our holy and God-bearing fathers, and all the saints, have mercy on us. Amen.

Prayer of Saint John Damascene, which is to be said while pointing at thy bed:

O Master, Lover of mankind, is this bed to be my coffin, or wilt Thou enlighten my wretched soul with another day? Behold, the coffin lieth before me; behold, death confronteth me. I fear, O Lord, Thy judgment and the endless torments, yet I cease not to do evil. My Lord God, I continually anger Thee, and Thy most pure Mother, and all the Heavenly Hosts, and my holy guardian angel. I know, O Lord, that I am unworthy of Thy love for mankind, but am worthy of every condemnation and torment. But, O Lord, whether I will it or not, save me. For to save a righteous man is no great thing, and to have mercy on the pure is nothing wonderful, for they are worthy of Thy mercy. But on me, a sinner, show the wonder of Thy mercy; in this reveal Thy love for mankind, lest my wickedness prevail over Thine ineffable goodness and merciful kindness; and order my life as Thou wilt.

And when about to lie down in bed, say this:

Enlighten mine eyes, O Christ God, lest at any time I sleep unto death, lest at any time mine enemy say: I have prevailed against him.

Glory to the Father, and to the Son, and to the Holy Spirit.

Be my soul's helper, O God, for I pass through the midst of many snares; deliver me out of them, and save me, O Good One, for Thou art the Lover of mankind.

Both now and ever, and unto the ages of ages. Amen.

The most glorious Mother of God,

more holy than the holy angels, let us hymn unceasingly with our hearts and mouths, confessing her to be the Theotokos, for truly she gaveth birth to God incarnate for us, and prayeth unceasingly for our souls.

Then kiss thy Cross, and make the sign of the Cross [with the Cross] from the head to the foot of the bed, and likewise from side to side, while saying the **Prayer to the Venerable Cross:**

L et God arise and let His enemies be scattered, and let them that hate Him flee from before His face. As smoke vanisheth, so let them vanish; as wax melteth before the fire, so let the demons perish from the presence of them that love God and who sign themselves with the sign of the Cross and say in gladness: Rejoice, most venerable and life-giving Cross of the Lord, for Thou drivest away the

demons by the power of our Lord
Jesus Christ Who was crucified on
thee, Who went down to hades and
trampled on the power of the devil,
and gave us thee, His venerable Cross,
for the driving away of every adversary. O most venerable and life-giving
Cross of the Lord, help me together
with the holy Lady Virgin Theotokos,
and with all the saints, unto the ages.
Amen.

Or:

Compass me about, O Lord, with
the power of Thy precious and life-giving Cross and preserve me from every
evil.

**Then, instead of [asking] forgive-
ness [of anyone else]:**

Remit, pardon, forgive, O God,
our offences, both voluntary and
involuntary, in word and deed, in
knowledge and ignorance, by day
and by night, in mind and thought;

forgive us all things, for Thou art good and the Lover of mankind.

Prayer:

O Lord, Lover of mankind, forgive them that hate and wrong us. Do good to them that do good. Grant our brethren and kindred their saving petitions and life eternal; visit the infirm and grant them healing. Guide those at sea. Journey with them that travel. Help Orthodox Christians to struggle. To them that serve and are kind to us grant remission of sins. On them that have charged us, the unworthy, to pray for them, have mercy according to Thy great mercy. Remember, O Lord, our fathers and brethren departed before us, and grant them rest where the light of Thy countenance shall visit them. Remember, O Lord, our brethren in captivity, and deliver them from every misfortune. Remember, O Lord, those that bear fruit and do good works in Thy holy churches, and grant them their saving petitions and life eternal. Remember also, O Lord, us Thy lowly and sinful and unworthy servants, and enlighten our minds with the light of Thy knowledge, and guide us in the way of Thy commandments; through the intercessions of our most pure Lady, the Theotokos and Ever-Virgin Mary, and of all Thy saints, for blessed art Thou unto the ages of ages. Amen.

Daily Confession of Sins:

I confess to Thee, my Lord God and Creator, in one Holy Trinity glorified and worshipped, to the Father, Son, and Holy Spirit, all my sins which I have committed in all the days of my life, and at every hour, at the present time and in the past, day and night, by deed, word, thought, gluttony, drunkenness, secret eating, idle talking, despondency, indolence, contradiction, disobedience, slandering, condemning, negligence, self-love, acquisitiveness, extortion, lying, dishonesty, mercenariness, jealousy, envy, anger, remembrance of wrongs, hatred, bribery; and by all my senses: sight, hearing, smell, taste, touch; and by the rest of my sins, of the soul together with the bodily, through which I have angered Thee, my God and Creator, and dealt unjustly with my neighbour. Sorrowing for these, I stand guilty before Thee, my God, but I have the will to repent. Only help me, O Lord my God, with tears I humbly entreat Thee. Forgive my past sins through Thy compassion, and absolve from all these which I have said in Thy presence, for Thou art good and the Lover of mankind.

When giving thyself up to sleep, say:

Into Thy hands, O Lord Jesus Christ my God, I commit my spirit. Do Thou bless me, do Thou have mercy on me, and grant me life eternal. Amen.

SELECTIONS FROM VESPERS
Verses from Psalm 103:
(Chanted at All-Night Vigil)

Bless the Lord, O my soul. Blessed art Thou, O Lord. Bless the Lord, O my soul. O Lord my God, Thou hast been magnified exceedingly.

Refrain: Blessed art Thou, O Lord.

Confession and majesty hast Thou put on.

Refrain: Blessed art Thou, O Lord.

Upon the mountains shall the waters stand.

Refrain: Wondrous are Thy works, O Lord.

Between the mountains will the waters run.

Refrain: Wondrous are Thy works, O Lord.

In wisdom hast Thou made them all, hast Thou made them all.

Refrain: Glory to Thee, O Lord, Who hast made them all, Who hast made them all.

Glory to the Father, and to the Son, and to the Holy Spirit, both now and ever, and unto the ages of ages. Amen.

Alleluia, alleluia, alleluia. Glory to Thee, O God. *Thrice.*

Verses from the First Kathisma:

Blessed is the man that hath not walked in the counsel of the ungodly. Alleluia, *thrice.*

For the Lord knoweth the way of the righteous, and the way of the ungodly shall perish. Alleluia, *thrice.*

Serve ye the Lord with fear, and

rejoice in Him with trembling. Alleluia, *thrice.*

Blessed are all that have put their
trust in Him. Alleluia, *thrice.*

Arise, O Lord, save me, O my God.
Alleluia, *thrice.*

Salvation is of the Lord, and Thy
blessing is upon Thy people. Alleluia,
thrice.

Glory to the Father, and to the Son,
and to the Holy Spirit, both now and
ever, and unto the ages of ages. Amen.
Alleluia, *thrice.*

Alleluia, alleluia, alleluia. Glory to
Thee, O God. *Thrice.*

Lord, I have cried:

Lord, I have cried unto Thee,
hearken unto me. Hearken unto
me, O Lord. Lord, I have cried unto
Thee, hearken unto me; attend to the
voice of my supplication, when I cry
unto Thee. Hearken unto me, O Lord.

Let my prayer be set forth as incense before Thee, the lifting up of my hands as an evening sacrifice. Hearken unto me, O Lord.

The Vesper Hymn to the Son of God:

O Gentle Light of the holy glory of the immortal, heavenly, holy, blessed Father, O Jesus Christ: Having come to the setting of the sun, having beheld the evening light, we praise the Father, the Son, and the Holy Spirit: God. Meet it is for Thee at all times to be hymned with reverent voices, O Son of God, Giver of life. Wherefore, the world doth glorify Thee.

Prayer at the Coming of Evening:

Vouchsafe, O Lord, to keep us this evening without sin. Blessed art Thou, O Lord, the God of our fathers, and praised and glorified is Thy name unto the ages. Amen.

Let Thy mercy, O Lord, be upon us, according as we have hoped in Thee. Blessed art Thou, O Lord, teach me Thy statutes. Blessed art Thou, O Master, give me understanding of Thy statutes. Blessed art Thou, O Holy One, enlighten me by Thy statutes.

O Lord, Thy mercy endureth for ever; disdain not the work of Thy hands. To Thee is due praise, to Thee is due a song, to Thee glory is due, to the Father, and to the Son, and to the Holy Spirit, now and ever, and unto the ages of ages. Amen.

The Prayer of St. Symeon:

Now lettest Thou Thy servant depart in peace, O Master, according to Thy word, for mine eyes have seen Thy salvation, which Thou hast prepared before the face of all peoples; a light of revelation for the Gentiles, and the glory of Thy people Israel.

Dismissal Troparia:

O Theotokos and Virgin, rejoice! O Mary, full of grace, the Lord is with thee; blessed art thou among women, and blessed is the Fruit of thy womb, for thou hast borne the Saviour of our souls.

On weekdays of Lent, also these:

Glory to the Father, and to the Son, and to the Holy Spirit.

O Baptizer of Christ, keep us all in remembrance, that we may be delivered from our iniquities; for to thee was given grace to intercede for us. *Prostration.*

Both now and ever, and unto the ages of ages. Amen.

Plead in our behalf, O holy apostles and all saints, that we may be delivered from perils and afflictions; for we have acquired you as fervent mediators before the Saviour. *Prostration.*

Beneath thy compassion do we take refuge, O Theotokos; disdain not our supplication in times of affliction; but do thou deliver us from perils, O only pure, O only blessed one. *Bow from the waist.*

SELECTIONS FROM MATINS
The Six Psalms

Glory to God in the highest, and on earth peace, good will among men. *Thrice.*

O Lord, Thou shalt open my lips, and my mouth shall declare Thy praise. *Twice.*

PSALM 3

O Lord, why are they multiplied that afflict me? Many rise up against me. Many say unto my soul: There is no salvation for him in his God. But Thou, O Lord, art my helper, my glory, and the lifter up of my head. I cried unto the Lord with my voice, and He heard me out of His holy mountain. I laid me down and slept; I awoke, for the Lord will help me. I will not be afraid of ten thousands of people that set themselves against me round about. Arise, O Lord, save me, O my God, for Thou hast smitten all who without cause are mine enemies; the teeth of sinners hast Thou broken. Salvation is of the Lord, and Thy blessing is upon Thy people.

I laid me down and slept; I awoke, for the Lord will help me.

PSALM 37

O Lord, rebuke me not in Thine anger, nor chasten me in Thy wrath. For Thine arrows are fastened in me, and Thou hast laid Thy hand heavily upon me. There is no healing in my flesh in the face of Thy wrath; and there is no peace in my bones in the face of my sins. For mine iniquities are risen higher than my head; as a heavy burden have they pressed heavily upon me. My bruises are become noisome and corrupt in the face of my folly. I have been wretched and utterly bowed down until the end; all the day long I went with downcast face. For my loins are filled with mockings, and there is no healing in my flesh. I am afflicted and humbled exceedingly, I have roared from the groaning of my heart. O Lord, before Thee is all my desire, and my groaning is not hid from Thee. My heart is troubled, my strength hath failed me; and the light of mine eyes, even this is not with me. My friends and my neighbours drew nigh over against me and stood, and my nearest of kin stood afar off. And they that sought after my soul used violence; and they that sought evils for me spake vain things, and craftinesses all the day long did they meditate. But as for me, like a deaf man I heard them not, and was as a speechless man that openeth not his mouth. And I became as a man that heareth not, and that hath in his mouth no reproofs. For in Thee have I hoped, O Lord, Thou wilt hearken unto me, O Lord my God. For I said: Let never mine enemies rejoice over me; yea, when my feet were shaken, those men spake boastful words against me. For I am ready for scourges, and my sorrow is continually before me. For I will declare mine iniquity, and I will take heed concerning my sin. But mine enemies live and are made stronger than I, and they that hated me unjustly are multiplied. They that render me evil for good slandered me, because I pursued goodness. Forsake me not, O Lord my God, depart not from me.

Be attentive unto my help, O Lord of my salvation.

Forsake me not, O Lord my God, depart not from me. Be attentive unto my help, O Lord of my salvation.

PSALM 62

O God, my God, unto Thee I rise early at dawn. My soul hath thirsted for Thee; how often hath my flesh longed after Thee in a land barren and untrodden and unwatered. So in the sanctuary have I appeared before Thee to see Thy power and Thy glory, For Thy mercy is better than lives; my lips shall praise Thee. So shall I bless Thee in my life, and in Thy name will I lift up my hands. As with marrow and fatness let my soul be filled, and with lips of rejoicing shall my mouth praise Thee. If I remembered Thee on my bed, at the dawn I meditated on Thee. For Thou art become my helper; in the shelter of Thy wings will I rejoice. My soul hath cleaved after Thee, Thy right hand hath been quick to help me. But as for these, in vain have they sought after my soul; they shall go into the nethermost parts of the earth, they shall be surrendered unto the edge of the sword; portions for foxes shall they be. But the king shall be glad in God, everyone shall be praised that sweareth by Him; for the mouth of them is stopped that speak unjust things.

At the dawn I meditated on Thee. For Thou art become my helper; in the shelter of Thy wings will I rejoice. My soul hath cleaved after Thee, Thy right hand hath been quick to help me.

Glory to the Father, and to the Son, and to the Holy Spirit, both now and ever, and unto the ages of ages. Amen.

Alleluia, alleluia, alleluia. Glory to Thee, O God. *Thrice.*

Lord, have mercy. *Thrice.*

Glory to the Father, and to the Son, and to the Holy Spirit, both now and ever, and unto the ages of ages. Amen.

PSALM 87

O Lord God of my salvation, by day have I cried and by night before Thee. Let my prayer come before Thee, bow down Thine ear unto my supplication. For filled with evils is my soul, and my life unto hades hath drawn nigh. I am counted with them that go down into the pit; I am become as a man without help, free among the dead, like the bodies of the slain that sleep in the grave, whom Thou rememberest no more, and they are cut off from Thy hand. They laid me in the lowest pit, in darkness and in the shadow of death. Against me is Thine anger made strong, and all Thy billows hast Thou brought upon me. Thou hast removed my friends afar from me; they have made me an abomination unto themselves. I have been delivered up, and have not come forth; mine eyes are grown weak from poverty. I have cried unto Thee, O Lord, the whole day long; I have stretched out my hands unto Thee. Nay, for the dead wilt Thou work wonders? Or shall physicians raise them up that they may give thanks unto Thee? Nay, shall any in the grave tell of Thy mercy, and of Thy truth in that destruction? Nay, shall Thy wonders be known in that darkness, and Thy righteousness in that land that is forgotten? But as for me, unto Thee, O Lord, have I cried; and in the morning shall my prayer come before Thee. Wherefore, O Lord, dost Thou cast off my soul and turnest Thy face away from me? A poor man am I, and in troubles from my youth; yea, having been exalted, I was humbled and brought to distress. Thy furies have passed upon me, and Thy terrors have sorely troubled me. They came round about me like water, all the day long they compassed me about together. Thou hast removed afar from me friend and neighbour, and mine acquaintances because of my misery.

O Lord God of my salvation, by day have I cried and by night before Thee. Let my prayer come before Thee, bow down Thine ear unto my supplication.

PSALM 102

Bless the Lord, O my soul, and all that is within me bless His holy name. Bless the Lord, O my soul, and forget not all that He hath done for thee, Who is gracious unto all thine iniquities, Who healeth all thine infirmities, Who redeemeth thy life from corruption, Who crowneth thee with mercy and compassion, Who fulfilleth thy desire with good things; thy youth shall be renewed as the eagle's. The Lord performeth deeds of mercy, and executeth judgment for all them that are wronged. He hath made His ways known unto Moses, unto the sons of Israel the things that He hath willed. Compassionate and merciful is the Lord, long-suffering and plenteous in mercy; not unto the end will He be angered, neither unto eternity will He be wroth. Not according to our iniquities hath He dealt with us, neither according to our sins hath He rewarded us. For according to the height of heaven from the earth, the Lord hath

made His mercy to prevail over them
that fear Him. As far as the east is from
the west, so far hath He removed our
iniquities from us. Like as a father
hath compassion upon his sons, so
hath the Lord had compassion upon
them that fear Him; for He knoweth
whereof we are made, He hath remembered that we are dust. As for man, his
days are as the grass; as a flower of the
field, so shall he blossom forth. For
when the wind is passed over it, then it
shall be gone, and no longer will it
know the place thereof. But the mercy
of the Lord is from eternity, even unto
eternity, upon them that fear Him.
And His righteousness is upon sons of
sons, upon them that keep His testament and remember His commandments to do them. The Lord in heav-
en hath prepared His throne, and His
kingdom ruleth over all. Bless the

Lord, all ye His angels, mighty in strength, that perform His word, to hear the voice of His words. Bless the Lord, all ye His hosts, His ministers that do His will. Bless the Lord, all ye His works, in every place of His dominion. Bless the Lord, O my soul.

In every place of His dominion, bless the Lord, O my soul.

PSALM 142

O Lord, hear my prayer, give ear unto my supplication in Thy truth; hearken unto me in Thy righteousness. And enter not into judgment with Thy servant, for in Thy sight shall no man living be justified. For the enemy hath persecuted my soul; he hath humbled my life down to the earth. He hath sat me in darkness as those that have been long dead, and my spirit within me is become despondent; within me my heart is troubled. I remembered days of old, I meditated on all Thy works, I pondered on the creations of Thy hands. I stretched forth my hands unto Thee; my soul thirsteth after Thee like a waterless land. Quickly hear me, O Lord, my spirit hath fainted away. Turn not Thy face away from me, lest I be like unto them that go down into the pit. Cause me to hear Thy mercy in the morning; for in Thee have I put my hope. Cause me to know, O Lord, the way wherein I should walk; for unto Thee have I lifted up my soul. Rescue me from mine enemies, O Lord; unto Thee have I fled for refuge. Teach me to do Thy will, for Thou art my God. Thy good Spirit shall lead me in the land of uprightness; for Thy name's sake, O Lord, shalt Thou quicken me. In Thy righteousness shalt Thou bring my soul out of affliction, and in Thy mercy shalt Thou utterly destroy mine enemies. And Thou shalt cut off all them that afflict my soul, for I am Thy servant.

Hearken unto me, O Lord, in Thy righteousness, and enter not into judgment with Thy servant. *Twice.*

Thy good Spirit shall lead me in the land of uprightness.

Glory to the Father, and to the Son, and to the Holy Spirit, both now and ever, and unto the ages of ages. Amen.

Alleluia, alleluia, alleluia. Glory to Thee, O God. *Thrice.*

After the Great Ectenia:

God is the Lord and hath appeared unto us. Blessed is he that cometh in the name of the Lord.

Then are sung the Troparia and the Theotokion as appointed.

The Polyeleos:

Praise ye the name of the Lord; O ye servants, praise the Lord. Alleluia, *thrice.*

Blessed is the Lord out of Sion, Who dwelleth in Jerusalem. Alleluia, *thrice.*

O give thanks unto the Lord, for He is good; for His mercy endureth for ever. Alleluia, *thrice.*

O give thanks unto the God of heaven; for His mercy endureth for ever. Alleluia, *thrice.*

Troparia of the Resurrection, Fifth Tone:

Blessed art Thou, O Lord, teach me Thy statutes.

The assembly of Angels was amazed, beholding Thee numbered among the dead; yet, O Saviour, destroying the stronghold of death, and with Thyself raising up Adam, and freeing all from hades.

Blessed art Thou, O Lord, teach me Thy statutes.

Why mingle ye myrrh with tears of pity, O ye women disciples? Thus the radiant angel within the tomb addressed the myrrh-bearing women; behold the tomb and understand, for the Saviour is risen from the tomb.

Blessed art Thou, O Lord, teach me Thy statutes.

Very early the myrrh-bearing women hastened unto Thy tomb, lamenting, but the angel stood before them and said: The time for lamentation is past, weep not, but tell of the Resurrection to the apostles.

Blessed art Thou, O Lord, teach me Thy statutes.

The myrrh-bearing women, with myrrh came to Thy tomb, O Saviour, bewailing, but the angel addressed them, saying: Why number ye the living among the dead, for as God He is risen from the tomb.

Glory to the Father, and to the Son, and to the Holy Spirit:

Let us worship the Father, and His Son, and the Holy Spirit, the Holy Trinity, one in essence, crying with the Seraphim: Holy, Holy, Holy art Thou, O Lord.

Both now and ever, and unto the ages of ages. Amen.

In bringing forth the Giver of Life, thou hast delivered Adam from sin, O Virgin, and hast brought joy to Eve instead of sorrow; and those fallen from life hath thereunto been restored, by Him Who of thee was incarnate, God and Man.

Alleluia, alleluia, alleluia. Glory to Thee, O God. *Thrice:*

The Hymns of Ascents,
Fourth Tone, First Antiphon:

From my youth do many passions war against me; but do Thou Thyself defend and save me, O my Saviour.

Ye haters of Sion, shall be shamed by the Lord; for like grass, by the fire shall ye be withered.

Glory to the Father, and to the Son, and to the Holy Spirit, both now and ever, and unto the ages of ages. Amen.

In the Holy Spirit, every soul is quickened, and through cleansing is exalted and made radiant by the Triple Unity in a hidden sacred manner.

The Resurrection Song
after the Gospel:

Having beheld the Resurrection of Christ, let us worship the holy Lord Jesus, the only sinless One. We worship Thy Cross, O Christ, and Thy holy

Resurrection we hymn and glorify. For Thou art our God, and we know none other beside Thee, we call upon Thy name. O come, all ye faithful, let us worship Christ's holy Resurrection, for behold, through the Cross joy hath come to all the world. Ever blessing the Lord, we hymn His Resurrection; for, having endured crucifixion, He hath destroyed death by death.

Glory to the Father, and to the Son, and to the Holy Spirit.

Through the prayers of the Apostles, O Merciful One, blot out the multitude of our transgressions.

Both now and ever, and unto the ages of ages. Amen.

Through the prayers of the Theotokos, O Merciful One, blot out the multitude of our transgressions.

Have mercy on me, O God, according to Thy great mercy; and according to the multitude of Thy compassions, blot out my transgression.

Jesus having risen from the grave, as He foretold, hath given us life eternal, and great mercy.

Before the Ninth Ode of the Canon, the Song of the Most Holy Theotokos:

My soul doth magnify the Lord, and my spirit hath rejoiced in God my Saviour.

Refrain: More honourable than the Cherubim and beyond compare more glorious than the Seraphim, who without corruption gavest birth to God the Word, the very Theotokos, thee do we magnify.

For He hath looked upon the lowliness of His handmaiden; for behold, from henceforth all generations shall call me blessed. *Refrain.*

For the Mighty One hath done

great things to me, and holy is His name; and His mercy is on them that fear Him unto generation and generation. *Refrain.*

He hath showed strength with His arm, He hath scattered the proud in the imagination of their heart. *Refrain.*

He hath put down the mighty from their seat, and exalted them of low degree; He hath filled the hungry with good things, and the rich He hath sent empty away. *Refrain.*

He hath holpen His servant Israel in remembrance of His mercy, as He spake to our fathers, to Abraham and his seed for ever. *Refrain.*

Theotokion:

[Sung on Sundays before the Doxology]

Most blessed art thou, O Virgin Theotokos, for through Him Who became incarnate of thee is hades led captive, Adam recalled, the curse annulled, Eve set free, death slain, and we are given life. Wherefore, we cry aloud in praise: Blessed art Thou, O Christ God, Who hast been thus well-pleased, glory to Thee.

The Great Doxology:

Glory to God in the highest, and on earth peace, good will among men. We praise Thee, we bless Thee, we worship Thee, we glorify Thee, we give thanks to Thee for Thy great glory. O Lord, Heavenly King, God the Father Almighty; O Lord, the Only-begotten Son, Jesus Christ; and O Holy Spirit. O Lord God, Lamb of God, Son of the Father, that takest away the sin of the world, have mercy on us; Thou that takest away the sins of the world, receive our prayer; Thou that sittest at the right hand of the Father, have mercy on us. For Thou only art holy, Thou only art the Lord, Jesus

Christ, to the glory of God the Father. Amen.

Every day will I bless Thee, and I will praise Thy name for ever, yea, for ever and ever.

Vouchsafe, O Lord, to keep us this day without sin. Blessed art Thou, O Lord, the God of our fathers, and praised and glorified is Thy name unto the ages. Amen.

Let Thy mercy, O Lord, be upon us, according as we have hoped in Thee.

Blessed art Thou, O Lord, teach me Thy statutes. *Thrice.*

Lord, Thou hast been our refuge in generation and generation. I said: O Lord, have mercy on me, heal my soul, for I have sinned against Thee. O Lord, unto Thee have I fled for refuge, teach me to do Thy will, for Thou art my God; for in Thee is the fountain of life, in Thy light shall we see light. O continue Thy mercy unto them that know Thee.

Holy God, Holy Mighty, Holy Immortal, have mercy on us. *Thrice.*

Glory to the Father, and to the Son, and to the Holy Spirit, both now and ever, and unto the ages of ages. Amen.

Holy Immortal, have mercy on us.

Holy God, Holy Mighty, Holy Immortal, have mercy on us.

Immediately after the Doxology:

Troparia of the Resurrection:

[Tones 1, 3, 5, and 7]

Today is salvation come unto the world; let us sing to Him Who arose from the tomb, and is the Author of our life. For having destroyed death by death, He hath given us the victory and great mercy.

[Tones 2, 4, 6, and 8]

Having risen from the tomb, and

having burst the bonds of hades, Thou hast destroyed the sentence of death, O Lord, delivering all from the snares of the enemy. Manifesting Thyself to Thine Apostles, Thou didst send them forth to preach; and through them hast granted Thy peace to the world, O Thou Who alone art plenteous in mercy.

THE DIVINE LITURGY
of
SAINT JOHN CHRYSOSTOM

Deacon: Bless, master.

Priest: Blessed is the kingdom of the Father, and of the Son, and of the Holy Spirit, now and ever, and unto the ages of ages.

Choir: Amen.

The Great Ectenia

Deacon: In peace let us pray to the Lord.

Choir: Lord, have mercy.

Deacon: For the peace from above, and the salvation of our souls, let us pray to the Lord.

Choir: Lord, have mercy.

Deacon: For the peace of the whole world, the good estate of the holy churches of God, and the union of all, let us pray to the Lord.

Choir: Lord, have mercy.

Deacon: For this holy temple, and for them that with faith, reverence, and the fear of God enter herein, let us pray to the Lord.

Choir: Lord, have mercy.

Deacon: For the Orthodox episcopate of the Church of Russia; for our lord the Very Most Reverend Metropolitan *N.,* First Hierarch of the Russian Church Abroad; for our lord the Most Reverend (Archbishop *or* Bishop *N., whose diocese it is*); for the venerable priesthood, the diaconate in Christ, for all the clergy and people, let us pray to the Lord.

Choir: Lord, have mercy.

Deacon: For the suffering Russian land and its Orthodox people both in the homeland and in the diaspora, and for their salvation, let us pray to the Lord.

Choir: Lord, have mercy.

Deacon: For this land, its authorities and armed forces, let us pray to the Lord.

Choir: Lord, have mercy.

Deacon: That He may deliver His people from enemies visible and invisible, and confirm in us oneness of mind, brotherly love, and piety, let us pray to the Lord.

Choir: Lord, have mercy.

Deacon: For this city, (*or* town, *or* holy monastery), for every city and country, and the faithful that dwell therein, let us pray to the Lord.

Choir: Lord, have mercy.

Deacon: For seasonable weather, abundance of the fruits of the earth, and peaceful times, let us pray to the Lord.

Choir: Lord, have mercy.

Deacon: For travelers by sea, land, and air; for the sick, the suffering, the imprisoned, and for their salvation, let us pray to the Lord.

Choir: Lord, have mercy.

Deacon: That we may be delivered from all tribulation, wrath, and necessity, let us pray to the Lord.

Choir: Lord, have mercy.

Deacon: Help us, save us, have mercy on us, and keep us, O God, by Thy grace.

Choir: Lord, have mercy.

Deacon: Calling to remembrance our most holy, most pure, most blessed, glorious Lady Theotokos and Ever-Virgin Mary with all the saints, let us commit ourselves and one another and all our life unto Christ our God.

Choir: To Thee, O Lord.

Priest: For unto Thee is due all

glory, honour, and worship: to the Father, and to the Son, and to the Holy Spirit, now and ever, and unto the ages of ages.

Choir: Amen.

The First Antiphon is chanted:

PSALM 102

Bless the Lord, O my soul; blessed art Thou, O Lord. Bless the Lord, O my soul, and all that is within me bless His holy name. Bless the Lord, O my soul, and forget not all that He hath done for thee, Who is gracious unto all thine iniquities, Who healeth all thine infirmities, Who redeemeth thy life from corruption, Who crowneth thee with mercy and compassion, Who fulfilleth thy desire with good things; thy youth shall be renewed as the eagle's. The Lord performeth deeds of mercy, and executeth judgment for all them that are wronged. He hath made His ways known unto Moses, unto the sons of Israel the things that He hath willed. Compassionate and merciful is the Lord, long-suffering and plenteous in mercy. Not unto the end will He be angered, neither unto eternity will He be wroth. Not according to our iniquities hath He dealt with us, neither according to our sins hath He rewarded us. For according to the height of heaven from the earth, the Lord hath made His mercy to prevail over them that fear Him. As far as the east is from the west, so far hath He removed our iniquities from us. Like as a father hath compassion upon His sons, so hath the Lord had compassion upon them that fear Him. For He knoweth whereof we are made, He hath remembered that we are dust. As for man, his days are as the grass; as a flower of the field, so shall he blossom forth. For when the wind is passed over it, then it shall be gone, and no longer will it know the place thereof. But the mercy of the Lord is from eternity, even unto eternity, upon them that fear Him. And His righteousness is upon sons of sons, upon them that keep His testament and remember His commandments to do them. The Lord in heaven hath prepared His throne, and His kingdom ruleth over all. Bless the Lord, all ye His angels, mighty in strength, that perform His word, to hear the voice of His words. Bless the Lord, all ye His hosts, His ministers that do His will. Bless the Lord, all ye His works, in every place of His dominion.

Glory to the Father, and to the Son, and to the Holy Spirit, both now and ever, and unto the ages of ages. Amen.

Bless the Lord, O my soul, and all that is within me, bless His holy name; blessed art Thou, O Lord.

On feasts special antiphons are chanted.

The Small Ectenia

Deacon: Again and again, in peace let us pray to the Lord.

Choir: Lord, have mercy.

Deacon: Help us, save us, have mercy on us, and keep us, O God, by Thy grace.

Choir: Lord, have mercy.

Deacon: Calling to remembrance our most holy, most pure, most blessed, glorious Lady Theotokos and Ever-Virgin Mary with all the saints, let us commit ourselves and one another and all our life unto Christ our God.

Choir: To Thee, O Lord.

Priest: For Thine is the dominion, and Thine is the kingdom, and the power, and the glory: of the Father, and of the Son, and of the Holy Spirit, now and ever, and unto the ages of ages.

Choir: Amen.

The Second Antiphon is chanted:

Glory to the Father, and to the Son, and to the Holy Spirit.

PSALM 145

Praise the Lord, O my soul. I will praise the Lord in my life, I will chant unto my God for as long as I have my being. Trust ye not in princes, in the sons of men, in whom there is no salvation. His spirit shall go forth, and he shall return unto his earth. In that day all his thoughts shall perish. Blessed is he of whom the God of Jacob is his help, whose hope is in the Lord his God, Who hath made heaven and the earth, the sea and all that is therein, Who keepeth truth unto eternity, Who executeth judgment for the wronged, Who giveth food unto the hungry. The Lord looseth the fettered; the Lord maketh wise the blind; the Lord setteth aright the fallen; the Lord loveth the righteous; the Lord preserveth the proselytes. He shall adopt for His own the orphan and widow, and the way of sinners shall He destroy. The Lord shall be king unto eternity; thy God, O Sion, unto generation and generation.

Both now and ever, and unto the ages of ages. Amen.

O Only-begotten Son and Word of God, Who art immortal, yet didst deign for our salvation to be incarnate of the holy Theotokos and Ever-Virgin Mary, and without change didst become man, and wast crucified, O Christ God, trampling down death by death, Thou Who art one of the Holy Trinity, glorified with the Father and the Holy Spirit, save us.

Deacon: Again and again, in peace let us pray to the Lord.

Choir: Lord, have mercy.

Deacon: Help us, save us, have mercy on us, and keep us, O God, by Thy grace.

Choir: Lord, have mercy.

Deacon: Calling to remembrance our most holy, most pure, most blessed, glorious Lady Theotokos and Ever-Virgin Mary with all the saints, let us commit ourselves and one another and all our life unto Christ our God.

Choir: To Thee, O Lord.

Priest: For a good God art Thou, and the Lover of mankind, and unto Thee do we send up glory: to the Father, and to the Son, and to the Holy Spirit, now and ever, and unto the ages of ages.

Choir: Amen.

Here the holy doors are opened for the Small Entry.

The Third Antiphon is chanted:

In Thy kingdom remember us, O Lord, when Thou comest in Thy kingdom.

Blessed are the poor in spirit, for theirs is the kingdom of heaven.

Blessed are they that mourn, for they shall be comforted.

Blessed are the meek, for they shall inherit the earth.

Blessed are they that hunger and thirst after righteousness, for they shall be filled.

Blessed are the merciful, for they shall obtain mercy.

Blessed are the pure in heart, for they shall see God.

Blessed are the peacemakers, for they shall be called sons of God.

Blessed are they that are persecuted for righteousness' sake, for theirs is the kingdom of heaven.

Blessed are ye when men shall revile you and persecute you, and shall say all manner of evil against you falsely for My sake.

Rejoice and be exceeding glad, for great is your reward in the heavens.

The Small Entry:

Deacon: Wisdom! Aright!

Choir: O come let us worship and fall down before Christ; O Son of God *(Sundays:* Who didst rise from the dead*) (on feasts of the Theotokos:* through the prayers of the Theotokos*) (On weekdays:* Who art wondrous in the saints*)*, save us who chant unto Thee: Alleluia.

Here are chanted the appointed troparia and kontakia.

Priest: For holy art Thou, O our

God, and unto Thee do we send up glory: to the Father, and to the Son, and to the Holy Spirit, now and ever: *(and if there be no deacon, at once:* and unto the ages of ages*)*.

Deacon: O Lord, save the pious, and hearken unto us.

Choir: O Lord, save the pious, and hearken unto us.

Deacon: And unto the ages of ages.

Choir: Amen. Holy God, Holy Mighty, Holy Immortal, have mercy on us. *Thrice.*

Glory to the Father, and to the Son, and to the Holy Spirit, both now and ever, and unto the ages of ages.

Holy Immortal, have mercy on us.

Holy God, Holy Mighty, Holy Immortal, have mercy on us.

Deacon: Let us attend.

Priest: Peace be unto all.

Reader : And to thy spirit.

Deacon: Wisdom!

Reader: The Prokeimenon in the ___Tone.

The choir chanteth the prokeimenon.

Deacon: Wisdom!

Reader: The Reading is from (the Acts of the Holy Apostles) *or:* (the Catholic Epistle of _____) *or* (the Epistle of the holy Apostle Paul to the ___, *or* to Timothy, *etc.*).

Deacon: Let us attend.

The reader readeth the Epistle. At the conclusion:

Priest: Peace be unto thee.

Reader : And to thy spirit.

Deacon: Wisdom!

Reader: Alleluia in the ___ Tone.

The choir chanteth the Alleluia.

Deacon: Bless, master, the bringer of the Good Tidings of the holy Apostle and Evangelist *N.*

Priest: May God, through the intercessions of the holy glorious, all-praised Apostle and Evangelist *N.*, give speech with great power unto thee that bringest good tidings, unto the fulfillment of the Gospel of His beloved Son, our Lord Jesus Christ.

Deacon: Amen.

Priest: Wisdom! Aright! Let us hear the Holy Gospel. Peace be unto all.

Choir: And to thy spirit.

Deacon: The Reading is from the Holy Gospel according to *N.*

Choir: Glory to Thee, O Lord, glory to Thee.

Deacon: Let us attend.

After the reading of the Holy Gospel:

Choir: Glory to Thee, O Lord, glory to Thee.

The Augmented Ectenia:

Deacon: Let us all say with our whole soul and with our whole mind, let us say.

Choir: Lord, have mercy.

Deacon: O Lord Almighty, the God of our fathers, we pray Thee, hearken and have mercy.

Choir: Lord, have mercy.

Deacon: Have mercy on us, O God, according to Thy great mercy, we pray Thee, hearken and have mercy.

Choir: Lord, have mercy. *Thrice.*

Deacon: Again we pray for the Orthodox episcopate of the Church of Russia; for our lord the Very Most Reverend Metropolitan *N.*, First Hierarch of the Russian Church Abroad; for our lord the Most Reverend (Archbishop *or* Bishop *N., whose diocese it is*); and all our brethren in Christ.

Choir: Lord, have mercy. *Thrice.*

Deacon: Again we pray for the suffering Russian land and its Orthodox people both in the homeland and in the diaspora and for their salvation.

Choir: Lord, have mercy. *Thrice.*

Deacon: Again we pray for this land, its authorities and armed forces.

Choir: Lord, have mercy. *Thrice.*

Deacon: Again we pray to the Lord our God that He may deliver His people from enemies visible and invisible, and confirm in us oneness of mind, brotherly love, and piety.

Choir: Lord, have mercy. *Thrice.*

Deacon: Again we pray for our brethren, the priests, priestmonks, and all our brethren in Christ.

Choir: Lord, have mercy. *Thrice.*

Deacon: Again we pray for the blessed and ever-memorable, holy Orthodox patriarchs; for pious kings and right-believing queens; and for the founders of this holy temple (*or* monastery), and for our fathers and brethren gone to their rest before us, and the Orthodox here and everywhere laid to rest.

Choir: Lord, have mercy. *Thrice.*

Here may be inserted other petitions.

Deacon: Again we pray for them that bring offerings and do good works in this holy and all-venerable temple; for them that minister and them that chant, and for all the people here present that await of Thee great and abundant mercy.

Choir: Lord, have mercy. *Thrice.*

Priest: For a merciful God art Thou, and the Lover of mankind, and unto Thee do we send up glory: to the Father, and to the Son, and to the Holy Spirit, now and ever, and unto the ages of ages.

Choir: Amen.

(Here should be inserted the Prayer for the Salvation of Russia.)

The Ectenia for the Departed
(Omitted on Sundays and feasts)

Deacon: Have mercy on us, O God, according to Thy great mercy, we pray Thee, hearken and have mercy.

Choir: Lord, have mercy. *Thrice.*

Deacon: Again we pray for the repose of the souls of the departed servants of God, *N., N.,* and that they may be forgiven every transgression, both voluntary and involuntary.

Choir: Lord, have mercy. *Thrice.*

Deacon: That the Lord God commit their souls to where the righteous repose.

Choir: Lord, have mercy. *Thrice.*

Deacon: The mercy of God, the kingdom of heaven, and the remission of their sins, let us ask of Christ the immortal King and our God.

Choir: Grant this, O Lord.

Deacon: Let us pray to the Lord.

Choir: Lord, have mercy.

Priest: For Thou art the resurrection, and the life, and the repose of Thy departed servants, *N., N.,* O Christ our God, and unto Thee do we send up glory, together with Thine unoriginate Father, and Thy Most-holy and good and life-creating Spirit, now and ever, and unto the ages of ages.

Choir: Amen.

The Ectenia for the Catechumens

Deacon: Pray, ye catechumens, to the Lord.

Choir: Lord, have mercy.

Deacon: Ye faithful, for the catechumens let us pray, that the Lord will have mercy on them.

Choir: Lord, have mercy.

Deacon: That He will catechize them with the word of Truth.

Choir: Lord, have mercy.

Deacon: That He will reveal unto them the Gospel of righteousness.

Choir: Lord, have mercy

Deacon: That He will unite them to His Holy, Catholic, and Apostolic Church.

Choir: Lord, have mercy.

Deacon: Save them, have mercy on them, help them, and keep them, O God, by Thy grace.

Choir: Lord, have mercy.

Deacon: Ye catechumens, bow your heads to the Lord.

Choir: To Thee, O Lord.

Priest: That they also with us may glorify Thy most honourable and majestic name: of the Father, and of the Son, and of the Holy Spirit, now and ever, and unto the ages of ages.

Choir: Amen.

The Ectenia of the Faithful

Deacon: As many as are catechumens, depart; catechumens, depart; as many as are catechumens, depart; let none of the catechumens remain; as many as are of the faithful, again and again, in peace let us pray to the Lord.

Choir: Lord, have mercy.

Deacon: Help us, save us, have mercy on us, and keep us, O God, by Thy grace.

Choir: Lord, have mercy.

Deacon: Wisdom!

Priest: For unto Thee is due all glory, honour, and worship: to the Father, and to the Son, and to the Holy Spirit, now and ever, and unto the ages of ages.

Choir: Amen.

Deacon: Again and again, in peace let us pray to the Lord.

Choir: Lord, have mercy.

If a priest serve without a deacon, the following four petitions are omitted.

Deacon: For the peace from above, and the salvation of our souls, let us pray to the Lord.

Choir: Lord, have mercy.

Deacon: For the peace of the whole world, the good estate of the holy churches of God, and the union of all, let us pray to the Lord

Choir: Lord, have mercy.

Deacon: For this holy temple, and for them that with faith, reverence, and the fear of God enter herein, let us pray to the Lord.

Choir: Lord, have mercy.

Deacon: That we may be delivered from all tribulation, wrath, and necessity, let us pray to the Lord.

Choir: Lord, have mercy.

———

Deacon: Help us, save us, have mercy on us, and keep us, O God, by Thy grace.

Choir: Lord, have mercy.

Deacon: Wisdom!

Priest: That always being guarded

under Thy dominion, we may send up glory unto Thee: to the Father, and to the Son, and to the Holy Spirit, now and ever, and unto the ages of ages.

Choir: Amen.

The Cherubic Hymn:

Choir: Let us who mystically represent the Cherubim, and chant the thrice-holy hymn unto the life-creating Trinity, now lay aside all earthly care.

The Great Entry:

Deacon: The Orthodox episcopate of the Church of Russia; our lord the Very Most Reverend *N.*, Metropolitan of Eastern America and New York, and First Hierarch of the Russian Church Abroad; and our lord the Most Reverend (Archbishop *or* Bishop *N., whose diocese it is*), may the Lord God remember in His kingdom, always, now and ever, and unto the ages of ages.

Priest: The suffering Russian land and its Orthodox people both in the homeland and in the diaspora, this land, its authorities and the faithful that dwell therein, may the Lord God remember in His kingdom, always, now and ever, and unto the ages of ages.

The clergy, the monastics, all that are persecuted and suffer for the Orthodox Faith; the founders, benefactors, and the brotherhood of this holy temple (*or* monastery), and all of you Orthodox Christians, may the Lord God remember in His kingdom, always, now and ever, and unto the ages of ages.

Choir: Amen. That we may receive the King of all, Who cometh invisibly upborne in triumph by the ranks of angels. Alleluia, alleluia, alleluia.

The Ectenia of Fervent Supplication

Deacon: Let us complete our prayer unto the Lord.

Choir: Lord, have mercy.

Deacon: For the venerable gifts set forth, let us pray to the Lord.

Choir: Lord, have mercy.

Deacon: For this holy temple, and for them that with faith, reverence, and the fear of God enter herein, let us pray to the Lord.

Choir: Lord, have mercy.

Deacon: That we may be delivered from all tribulation, wrath, and necessity, let us pray to the Lord.

Choir: Lord, have mercy.

Deacon: Help us, save us, have mercy on us, and keep us, O God, by Thy grace.

Choir: Lord, have mercy.

Deacon: That the whole day may be perfect, holy, peaceful, and sinless, let us ask of the Lord.

Choir: Grant this, O Lord.

Deacon: An angel of peace, a faithful guide, a guardian of our souls and bodies, let us ask of the Lord.

Choir: Grant this, O Lord.

Deacon: Pardon and remission of our sins and offences, let us ask of the Lord.

Choir: Grant this, O Lord.

Deacon: Things good and profitable for our souls, and peace for the world, let us ask of the Lord.

Choir: Grant this, O Lord.

Deacon: That we may complete the remaining time of our life in peace and repentance, let us ask of the Lord.

Choir: Grant this, O Lord.

Deacon: A Christian ending to our life, painless, blameless, peaceful, and a good defense before the dread judgment seat of Christ, let us ask.

Choir: Grant this, O Lord.

Deacon: Calling to remembrance our most holy, most pure, most blessed, glorious Lady Theotokos and Ever Virgin Mary with all the saints, let us commit ourselves and one another and all our life unto Christ our God.

Choir: To Thee, O Lord.

Priest: Through the compassions of Thine Only-begotten Son, with Whom Thou art blessed, together with Thy Most-holy, and good, and life-creating Spirit, now and ever, and unto the ages of ages.

Choir: Amen.

Priest: Peace be unto all.

Choir: And to thy spirit.

Deacon: Let us love one another, that with one mind we may confess:

Choir: The Father, and the Son, and the Holy Spirit: the Trinity, one in essence and indivisible.

Deacon: The doors! The doors! In wisdom let us attend.

The Symbol of Faith:

I believe in one God, the Father Almighty, Maker of heaven and earth, and of all things visible and invisible. And in one Lord Jesus Christ, the Son of God, the Only-begotten, begotten of the Father before all ages; Light of Light, true God of true God; begotten, not made; of one essence with the Father; by Whom all things were made; Who for us men, and for our salvation, came down from the heavens, and was incarnate of the Holy Spirit and the Virgin Mary, and became man; And was crucified for us under Pontius Pilate, and suffered, and was buried; and arose again on the third day according to the Scriptures; And ascended into the heavens, and sitteth at the right hand of the Father;

And shall come again, with glory, to judge both the living and the dead; Whose kingdom shall have no end. And in the Holy Spirit, the Lord, the Giver of life; Who proceedeth from the Father; Who with the Father and the Son together is worshipped and glorified; Who spake by the prophets. In One, Holy, Catholic, and Apostolic Church. I confess one baptism for the remission of sins. I look for the resurrection of the dead, And the life of the age to come. Amen.

The Anaphora:

Deacon: Let us stand well. let us stand with fear, let us attend, that we may offer the holy oblation in peace.

Choir: A mercy of peace, a sacrifice of praise.

Priest: The grace of our Lord Jesus Christ, and the love of God the Father, and the communion of the Holy Spirit be with you all.

Choir: And with thy spirit.

Priest: Let us lift up our hearts.

Choir: We lift them up unto the Lord.

Priest: Let us give thanks unto the Lord.

Choir: It is meet and right to worship the Father, and the Son, and the Holy Spirit: the Trinity, one in essence and indivisible.

Priest: Singing the triumphal hymn, shouting, crying aloud, and saying:

Choir: Holy, Holy, Holy, Lord of Sabaoth: heaven and earth are full of Thy glory. Hosanna in the highest! Blessed is He that cometh in the name of the Lord. Hosanna in the highest!

If it be the Liturgy of Saint John Chrysostom:

Priest: Take, eat: this is My Body,

which is broken for you for the remission of sins.

Choir: Amen.

Priest: Drink of it, all of you: this is My Blood of the New Testament, which is shed for you and for many, for the remission of sins.

Choir: Amen.

But if it be the Liturgy of Saint Basil the Great:

Priest: He gave it to His holy disciples and apostles, saying: Take, eat: this is My Body, which is broken for you for the remission of sins.

Choir: Amen.

Priest: He gave it to His holy disciples and apostles, saying: Drink of it, all of you: this is My Blood of the New Testament, which is shed for you and for many, for the remission of sins.

Choir: Amen.

Priest: Thine Own of Thine Own we

offer unto Thee, in behalf of all and for all.

Choir: We praise Thee, we bless Thee, we give thanks unto Thee, O Lord; and we pray unto Thee, O our God.

Priest: Especially for our most holy, most pure, most blessed, glorious Lady Theotokos and Ever-Virgin Mary.

If it be the Liturgy of Saint John Chrysostom:

Choir: It is truly meet to bless thee, the Theotokos, ever-blessed and most-blameless, and Mother of our God. More honourable than the Cherubim, and beyond compare more glorious than the Seraphim, who without corruption gavest birth to God the Word, the very Theotokos, thee do we magnify.

If it be the Liturgy of Saint Basil the Great:

Choir: In thee rejoiceth, O thou who art full of grace, all creation, the angelic assembly, and the race of man; O sanctified temple and noetical paradise, praise of virgins, of whom God was incarnate, and became a child, He that was before the ages, even our God; for of thy body a throne He made, and thy womb more spacious than the heavens did He form. In thee rejoiceth, O thou who art full of grace, all creation: glory to thee.

Priest: Among the first, remember, O Lord the Orthodox episcopate of the Church of Russia; and our lord the Very Most Reverend Metropolitan *N.*, First Hierarch of the Russian Church Abroad; and our lord the Most Reverend (Archbishop *or* Bishop *N. whose diocese it is*), whom do Thou grant unto Thy holy churches, in peace, safety, honour, health, and length of days, rightly dividing the word of Thy truth.

Choir: And each and every one.

Priest: And grant unto us that with one mouth and one heart we may glorify and hymn Thy most honourable and majestic name: of the Father, and of the Son, and of the Holy Spirit, now and ever, and unto the ages of ages.

Choir: Amen.

Priest: And may the mercies of our great God and Saviour Jesus Christ be with you all.

Choir: And with thy spirit.

Deacon: Having called to remembrance all the saints, again and again, in peace let us pray to the Lord.

Choir: Lord, have mercy.

Deacon: For the venerable Gifts offered and sanctified, let us pray to the Lord.

Choir: Lord, have mercy.

Deacon: That our God, the Lover of mankind, having accepted them upon His holy and most heavenly and noetic altar as an odour of spiritual fragrance, will send down upon us divine grace and the gift of the Holy Spirit, let us pray.

Choir: Lord, have mercy.

Deacon: That we may be delivered from all tribulation, wrath, and necessity, let us pray to the Lord.

Choir: Lord, have mercy.

Deacon: Help us, save us, have mercy on us, and keep us, O God, by Thy grace.

Choir: Lord, have mercy.

Deacon: That the whole day may be perfect, holy, peaceful, and sinless, let us ask of the Lord.

Choir: Grant this, O Lord.

Deacon: An angel of peace, a faithful guide, a guardian of our souls and bodies, let us ask of the Lord.

Choir: Grant this, O Lord.

Deacon: Pardon and remission of our sins and offences, let us ask of the Lord.

Choir: Grant this, O Lord.

Deacon: Things good and profitable for our souls, and peace for the world, let us ask of the Lord.

Choir: Grant this, O Lord.

Deacon: That we may complete the remaining time of our life in peace and repentance, let us ask of the Lord.

Choir: Grant this, O Lord.

Deacon: A Christian ending to our life, painless, blameless, peaceful, and a good defence before the dread judgment seat of Christ, let us ask.

Choir: Grant this, O Lord.

Deacon: Having asked for the unity of the faith and the communion of the Holy Spirit, let us commit ourselves and one another and all our life unto Christ our God.

Choir: To Thee, O Lord.

Priest: And vouchsafe us, O Master, that with boldness and without condemnation we may dare to call upon Thee the heavenly God as Father, and to say:

Choir/People: Our Father, Who art in the heavens, hallowed be Thy name. Thy kingdom come, Thy will be done, on earth as it is in heaven. Give us this day our daily bread; and forgive us our debts, as we forgive our debtors; and lead us not into temptation, but deliver us from the evil one.

Priest: For Thine is the kingdom, and the power, and the glory: of the Father, and of the Son, and of the Holy Spirit, now and ever, and unto the ages of ages.

Choir: Amen.

Priest: Peace be unto all.

Choir: And to thy spirit.

Deacon: Bow your heads unto the Lord.

Choir: To Thee, O Lord.

Priest: Through the grace and compassions and love for mankind of Thine Only-begotten Son, with Whom Thou art blessed, together with Thy Most-holy and good and life-creating Spirit, now and ever, and unto the ages of ages.

Choir: Amen.

Deacon: Let us attend!

Priest: Holy Things are for the holy.

Choir: One is Holy, One is Lord, Jesus Christ, to the glory of God the Father. Amen.

And the choir chanteth the Communion Verse: Praise the Lord from the heavens, praise Him in the highest. Alleluia, alleluia, alleluia.

After the communion of the clergy:

Deacon: With fear of God and with faith draw nigh.

Choir: Blessed is He that cometh in the name of the Lord. God is the Lord, and hath appeared unto us.

Priest: I believe, O Lord, and I confess that Thou art truly the Christ, the Son of the living God, Who didst come into the world to save sinners of whom I am chief. Moreover, I believe that this is truly Thy most pure Body, and that this is truly Thine Own venerable Blood. Wherefore, I pray Thee: Have mercy on me and forgive me my transgressions, voluntary and involuntary, in word and deed, in knowledge and in ignorance. And vouchsafe me to partake without condemnation of Thy most pure Mysteries unto the remission of sins and life everlasting. Amen.

Of Thy Mystical Supper, O Son of God, receive me today as a communicant; for I will not speak of the Mystery to Thine enemies, nor will I give Thee a kiss as did Judas, but like the Thief do I confess Thee: Remember me, O Lord, in Thy kingdom.

Let not the communion of Thy holy Mysteries be unto me for judgment or condemnation O Lord, but for healing of soul and body.

And as each person receiveth Holy Communion, the priest (bishop) saith:

The servant (*or* handmaid) of God, *N.*, partaketh of the venerable and holy Body and Blood of our Lord God and Saviour Jesus Christ, unto the remission of sins and life everlasting.

Choir: Receive ye the Body of Christ; taste ye of the Fountain of Immortality.

When all communicants have received:

Alleluia, alleluia. alleluia.

Priest: Save, O God, Thy people and bless Thine inheritance.

Choir: We have seen the True Light, we have received the Heavenly Spirit, we have found the True Faith, we worship the indivisible Trinity: for He hath saved us.

Priest: Always, now and ever, and unto the ages of ages.

Choir: Amen. Let our mouth be filled with Thy praise, O Lord, that we may hymn Thy glory, for Thou hast vouchsafed us to partake of Thy holy, divine, immortal, and life-creating Mysteries. Keep us in Thy holiness, that we may meditate on Thy righteousness all the day long. Alleluia, alleluia, alleluia.

Deacon: Aright! Having partaken of the divine, holy, most pure, immortal, heavenly, and life-creating, fearful

Mysteries of Christ, let us worthily give thanks unto the Lord.

Choir: Lord, have mercy.

Deacon: Help us, save us, have mercy on us, and keep us, O God, by Thy grace.

Choir: Lord, have mercy.

Deacon: Having asked that the whole day may be perfect, holy, peaceful, and sinless, let us commit ourselves and one another and all our life unto Christ our God.

Choir: To Thee, O Lord.

Priest: For Thou art our sanctification, and unto Thee do we send up glory: to the Father, and to the Son, and to the Holy Spirit, now and ever, and unto the ages of ages.

Choir: Amen.

Deacon: In peace let us depart.

Choir: In the name of the Lord.

Deacon: Let us pray to the Lord.

Choir: Lord, have mercy.

*Priest, the **Prayer below the Ambo:***

O Lord Who dost bless them that bless Thee and sanctify them that put their trust in Thee: Save Thy people and bless Thine inheritance; preserve the fullness of Thy Church, sanctify them that love the beauty of Thy house; do Thou glorify them by Thy divine power, and forsake us not that hope in Thee. Give peace to Thy world, to Thy churches, to the priests, and to all Thy people. For every good gift and every perfect gift is from above, and cometh down from Thee, the Father of lights, and unto Thee do we send up glory and thanksgiving and worship: to the Father, and to the Son, and to the Holy Spirit, now and ever, and unto the ages of ages.

Choir: Amen. Blessed be the name of the Lord from henceforth and for evermore. *Thrice.*

Priest: The blessing of the Lord be upon you, through His grace and love for mankind, always, now and ever, and unto the ages of ages.

Choir: Amen.

Priest: Glory to Thee, O Christ God, our hope, glory to Thee.

Choir: Glory to the Father, and to the Son, and to the Holy Spirit, both now and ever, and unto the ages of ages. Amen.

Lord, have mercy. *Thrice.*

Father (Master), bless.

Priest: May Christ our true God, *(On Sundays:* Who rose from the dead*)*, through the intercessions of His most pure Mother, of the holy and glorious apostles, of our father among the saints, John Chrysostom, archbishop of Constantinople (*or* Basil the Great, archbishop of Caesarea in Cappadocia), and Saint(s) *N.(N.) (whose temple it is),* and Saint(s) *N.(N.) (whose day it is),* of the holy and Righteous Ancestors of God, Joachim and Anna, and of all the saints: have mercy on us and save us, for He is good and the Lover of mankind.

Choir: Amen. *And the* Many Years:

The End of the Divine Liturgy

Sunday Troparia and Kontakia

FIRST TONE:

Troparion: When the stone had been sealed by the Jews, and the soldiers were guarding Thine immaculate Body, Thou didst arise on the third day, O Saviour, granting life unto the world. Wherefore, the Hosts of the heavens cried out to Thee, O Life-giver: Glory to Thy Resurrection, O Christ. Glory to Thy kingdom. Glory to Thy dispensation, O only Lover of mankind.

Kontakion: As God, Thou didst arise from the tomb in glory, and Thou didst raise the world together with Thyself. And mortal nature praiseth Thee as God, and death hath vanished. And Adam danceth, O Master, and Eve, now freed from fetters, rejoiceth as she crieth out: Thou art He, O Christ, that grantest unto all resurrection.

SECOND TONE:

Troparion: When Thou didst descend unto death, O Life Immortal, then didst Thou slay hades with the lightning of Thy Divinity. And when Thou didst also raise the dead out of the nethermost depths, all the Hosts of the heavens cried out: O Life-giver, Christ our God, glory be to Thee.

Kontakion: Thou didst arise from the tomb, O omnipotent Saviour, and hades was terrified on beholding the wonder; and the dead arose, and creation at the sight thereof rejoiceth with Thee. And Adam also is joyful, and the world, O my Saviour, praiseth Thee for ever.

THIRD TONE:

Troparion: Let the heavens be glad; let earthly things rejoice; for the Lord hath wrought might with His arm. He hath trampled down death by death; the firstborn of the dead hath He become. From the belly of hades hath He delivered us and hath granted to the world great mercy.

Kontakion: Thou didst arise today from the tomb, O Merciful One, and didst lead us out of the gates of death. Today Adam danceth and Eve rejoiceth; and together with them both the Prophets and the Patriarchs unceasingly praise the divine might of Thine authority.

FOURTH TONE:

Troparion: Having learned the joyful proclamation of the Resurrection from the angel, and having cast off the ancestral condemnation, the women disciples of the Lord spake to the apostles exultantly: Death is despoiled and Christ God is risen, granting to the world great mercy.

Kontakion: My Saviour and Redeemer hath, as God, raised up the earthborn from the grave and from their fetters, and He hath broken the gates of hades, and, as Master, hath risen on the third day.

FIFTH TONE:

Troparion: Let us, O faithful, praise and worship the Word Who is co-unoriginate with the Father and the Spirit, and Who was born of the Virgin for our salvation; for He was pleased to ascend the Cross in the flesh and to endure death, and to raise the dead by His glorious Resurrection.

Kontakion: Unto hades, O my Saviour, didst Thou descend, and having broken its gates as One omnipotent, Thou, as Creator, didst raise up the dead together with Thyself. And Thou didst break the sting of death, and didst deliver Adam from the curse, O Lover of mankind. Wherefore, we all cry unto Thee: Save us, O Lord.

SIXTH TONE:

Troparion: Angelic Hosts were above Thy tomb, and they that guarded Thee became as dead. And Mary stood by the grave seeking Thine immaculate Body. Thou didst despoil hades and wast not tempted by it. Thou didst meet the Virgin and didst grant us life. O Thou Who didst rise from the dead, O Lord, glory be to Thee.

Kontakion: Having by His life-bestowing hand raised up all the dead out of the dark abysses, Christ God, the Giver of Life, hath bestowed the Resurrection upon the fallen human race; for He is the Saviour of all, the Resurrection, and the Life, and the God of all.

SEVENTH TONE:

Troparion: Thou didst destroy death by Thy Cross, Thou didst open Paradise to the thief. Thou didst change the lamentation of the Myrrh-bearers, and Thou didst command Thine Apostles to proclaim that Thou didst arise, O Christ God, and grantest to the world great mercy.

Kontakion: No longer will the dominion of death be able to keep men captive; for Christ hath descended, demolishing and destroying the powers thereof. Hades is bound; the Prophets rejoice with one voice, saying: A

Saviour hath come for them that have faith. Come forth, ye faithful, for the Resurrection.

EIGHTH TONE:

Troparion: From on high didst Thou descend, O Compassionate One; to burial of three days hast Thou submitted that Thou mightest free us from our passions. O our Life and Resurrection, O Lord, glory be to Thee.

Kontakion: Having arisen from the tomb, Thou didst raise up the dead and didst resurrect Adam. Eve also danceth at Thy Resurrection, and the ends of the world celebrate Thine arising from the dead, O Greatly-merciful One.

Daily Troparia and Kontakia

MONDAY—The Bodiless Hosts:

Troparion, Fourth Tone: Supreme Commanders of the heavenly hosts, we unworthy ones implore you that by your supplications ye will encircle us with the shelter of the wings of your immaterial glory, and guard us who fall down before you and fervently cry: Deliver us from dangers since ye are the Marshalls of the Hosts on high.

Kontakion, Second Tone: Supreme Commanders of God and ministers of the Divine Glory, guides of men and leaders of the angels, ask for what is to our profit and for great mercy, since ye are the Supreme Commanders of the Bodiless Hosts.

TUESDAY—St. John the Forerunner:
Troparion, Second Tone: The memory of the righteous is celebrated with hymns of praise, but the Lord's testimony is sufficient for thee, O Forerunner; for thou hast proved to be truly even more venerable than the prophets, since thou wast granted to baptize in the running waters Him Whom they proclaimed. Wherefore, having contested for the truth, thou didst rejoice to announce the good tidings even to those in hades: that God hath appeared in the flesh, taking away the sin of the world and granting us great mercy.

Kontakion, Second Tone: O Prophet of God and Forerunner of grace, having obtained thy head from the earth as a most sacred rose, we ever receive healings; for again, as of old in the world, thou preachest repentance.

WEDNESDAY and FRIDAY— the Cross:

Troparion, First Tone: Save, O Lord, Thy people, and bless Thine inheritance; grant Thou unto Orthodox Christians victory over enemies; and by the power of Thy Cross do Thou preserve Thy commonwealth.

Kontakion, Fourth Tone: O Thou Who wast lifted up willingly on the Cross, bestow Thy mercies upon the new community named after Thee, O Christ God; gladden with Thy power the Orthodox Christians, granting them victory over enemies; may they have as Thy help the weapon of peace, the invincible trophy.

THURSDAY— the Holy Apostles, and Saint Nicholas:

Troparion to the Apostles, Third Tone: O holy Apostles, intercede with the merciful God, that He grant unto our souls forgiveness of offences.

Troparion to Saint Nicholas, Fourth Tone: The truth of things revealed thee to thy flock as a rule of faith, an icon of meekness and a teacher of temperance; therefore thou hast achieved the heights by humility, riches by poverty. O Father and Hierarch Nicholas, intercede with Christ God that our souls be saved.

Kontakion to the Holy Apostles, Second Tone: The firm and divine-voiced preachers, the chief of Thy disciples, O Lord, Thou hast taken to Thyself for the enjoyment of Thy blessings and for repose; their labours and death didst Thou accept as above every sacrifice, O Thou Who alone knowest the hearts.

Kontakion to Saint Nicholas, Third Tone: In Myra, O Saint, thou didst prove to be a minister of things sacred:

for having fulfilled the Gospel of Christ, O righteous one, thou didst lay down thy life for thy people, and didst save the innocent from death. Wherefore, thou wast sanctified, as a great initiate of the grace of God.

SATURDAY—All Saints, and the Departed:

Troparion to All Saints, Second Tone: O Apostles, Martyrs, and Prophets, Hierarchs, Monastics, and Righteous Ones; ye that have accomplished a good labour and kept the Faith, that have boldness before the Saviour; O Good Ones, intercede for us, we pray, that our souls be saved.

Troparion for the Departed, Eighth Tone: O Thou Who by the depth of Thy wisdom, out of love for mankind, dost provide all things, and grantest unto all that which is profitable, O only Creator: Grant rest, O Lord, to the souls of Thy servants, for in Thee have they placed their hope, O our Creator and Fashioner and God.

Kontakion for the Departed, Eighth Tone: With the saints give rest, O Christ, to the souls of Thy servants, where there is neither sickness, nor sorrow, nor sighing, but life everlasting.

Kontakion to the Martyrs, Eighth Tone: To Thee, O Lord, the Planter of creation, the world doth offer the God-bearing martyrs as the firstfruits of nature. By their intercessions preserve Thy Church, Thy commonwealth, in profound peace, through the Theotokos, O Greatly-merciful One.

Troparia and Kontakia of the Immovable Great Feasts

The Nativity of the Most Holy Theotokos

Troparion, Fourth Tone:

Thy nativity, O Theotokos Virgin,* hath proclaimed joy to all the world;* for from thee hath dawned the Sun of Righteousness, Christ our God,* annulling the curse and bestowing the blessing,* abolishing death and granting us life eternal.

Kontakion, Fourth Tone:

Joachim and Anna were freed from the reproach of childlessness* and Adam and Eve from the corruption of death, by thy holy nativity, O immaculate one,* which thy people, redeemed from the guilt of offences,* celebrate by crying to thee:* The barren woman giveth birth to the Theotokos, the nourisher of our life.

The Elevation of the Precious and Life-giving Cross of the Lord
Troparion, First Tone:

Save, O Lord, Thy people,* and bless Thine inheritance;* grant Thou unto Orthodox Christians victory over enemies;* and by the power of Thy Cross do Thou preserve Thy commonwealth.

Kontakion, Fourth Tone:

O Thou Who wast lifted up willingly on the Cross,* bestow Thy mercies upon the new community named after Thee, O Christ God;* gladden with Thy power the Orthodox Christians,* granting them victory over enemies;* may they have as Thy help the weapon of peace, the invincible trophy.

The Entry of Our Most Holy Lady Theotokos and Ever-Virgin Mary into the Temple
Troparion, Fourth Tone:

Today is the prelude of God's good-will* and the heralding of the salvation of mankind.* In the temple of God, the Virgin is presented openly,* and she proclaimeth Christ unto all.* To her, then, with a great voice let us cry aloud:* Rejoice, O thou fulfillment* of the Creator's dispensation.

Kontakion, Fourth Tone:

The most pure temple of the Saviour,* the most precious bridal-chamber and Virgin,* the sacred treasury of the glory of God,* is on this day brought into the house of the Lord,* bringing with her the grace that is in the Divine Spirit.* And the angels of God chant praise unto her:* she is the heavenly tabernacle.

The Nativity of Our Lord God and Saviour Jesus Christ
Troparion, Fourth Tone:

Thy Nativity, O Christ our God,* hath shined upon the world the light of knowledge;* for thereby, they that worshipped the stars* were taught by a star* to worship Thee, the Sun of Righteousness,* and to know Thee, the Dayspring from on high.* O Lord, glory be to Thee.

Kontakion, Third Tone:

Today the Virgin giveth birth to Him Who is transcendent in essence;* and the earth offereth a cave to Him Who is unapproachable.* Angels with shepherds give glory;* with a star the Magi do journey;* for our sake a young Child is born, Who is pre-eternal God.

The Theophany of our Lord God and Saviour Jesus Christ
Troparion, First Tone:

When Thou wast baptized in the Jordan, O Lord,* the worship of the Trinity was made manifest;* for the voice of the Father bare witness to Thee,* calling Thee His beloved Son.* And the Spirit in the form of a dove* confirmed the certainty of the world.* O Christ our God, Who hast appeared* and hast enlightened the world, glory be to Thee.

Kontakion, Fourth Tone:

Thou hast appeared today unto the whole world,* and Thy light, O Lord, hath been signed upon us* who with knowledge chant unto Thee:* Thou hast come, Thou hast appeared,* O Light Unapproachable.

The Meeting of the Lord
Troparion, First Tone:

Rejoice, thou who art full of grace, O Virgin Theotokos,* for from thee hath risen the Sun of Righteousness, Christ our God,* enlightening those in darkness.* Rejoice, thou also, O righteous Elder,* as thou receivest in thine arms the Redeemer of our souls,* Who also granteth unto us the Resurrection.

Kontakion, First Tone:

Thou who didst sanctify the Virgin's womb by Thy birth,* and didst bless Symeon's hands as was meet,* by anticipation didst even now save us, O Christ God.* But grant peace in the midst of wars unto Thy commonwealth,* and strengthen Orthodox Christians* whom Thou hast loved, O only Lover of mankind.

The Annunciation
of the Most Holy Theotokos
Troparion, Fourth Tone:

Today is the fountainhead of our salvation* and the manifestation of the mystery which was from eternity.* The Son of God becometh the Virgin's Son,* and Gabriel proclaimeth the good tidings of grace;* wherefore, we also cry to the Theotokos with him:* Rejoice, thou who art full of grace,* the Lord is with thee.

Kontakion, Eighth Tone:

To thee, the Champion Leader, we thy servants dedicate a feast of victory and of thanksgiving* as ones rescued out of sufferings, O Theotokos;* but as thou art one with might which is invincible,* from all dangers that can be do thou deliver us, that we may cry to thee:* Rejoice, thou Bride Unwedded.

The Transfiguration of the Lord
Troparion, Seventh Tone:

Thou wast transfigured on the mountain, O Christ our God,* showing to Thy disciples Thy glory as each one could endure;* shine forth Thou on us, who are sinners all, Thy light ever-unending* through the prayers of the Theotokos. O Light-giver, glory to Thee.

Kontakion, Seventh Tone:

On the mount Thou wast trans-figured,* and Thy disciples, as much as they could bear, beheld Thy glory, O Christ God;* so that when they should see Thee crucified,* they would know Thy passion to be willing,* and would preach to the world* that Thou, in truth, art the Effulgence of the Father.

The Dormition
of The Most Holy Theotokos
Troparion, First Tone:

In giving birth thou didst preserve thy virginity;* in thy dormition thou didst not forsake the world, O Theotokos.* Thou wast translated unto life,* since thou art the Mother of Life;* and by thine intercessions dost thou deliver our souls from death.

Kontakion, Second Tone:

The grave and death could not hold the Theotokos,* who is sleepless in her intercessions and an unfailing hope in her mediations.* For as the Mother of Life she was translated unto life* by Him Who dwelt in her ever-virgin womb.

Troparia, Kontakia, Prayers, and Stichera from the Triodion

THE SUNDAY OF THE PUBLICAN AND THE PHARISEE

After the Matins Gospel, **Eighth Tone:**

The doors of repentance do Thou open to me, O Giver of life, for my spirit waketh at dawn toward Thy holy temple, bearing a temple of the body all defiled. But in Thy compassion, cleanse it by the loving-kindness of Thy mercy.

Theotokion: Guide me in the paths of salvation, O Theotokos, for I have defiled my soul with shameful sins, and have wasted all my life in slothfulness, but by thine intercessions deliver me from all uncleanness.

Sixth Tone: Have mercy on me, O God, according to Thy great mercy; and according to the multitude of Thy compassions, blot out my transgression.

When I think of the multitude of evil things I have done, I, a wretched one, I tremble at the fearful day of judgment; but trusting in the mercy of Thy loving-kindness, like David do I cry unto Thee: Have mercy on me, O God, according to Thy great mercy.

[Note: These penitential songs the Church chanteth on the Sunday of the Publican and the Pharisee and the Sundays thereafter through the Fifth Sunday of Great Lent.]

Kontakion, Fourth Tone: Let us flee the bragging of the Pharisee, and learn the humility of the Publican, while crying out unto the Saviour with groanings: Be gracious unto us, O Thou Who alone dost readily forgive.

THE SUNDAY
OF THE PRODIGAL SON

Kontakion, Third Tone: Having foolishly abandoned Thy paternal glory, I squandered on vices the wealth which Thou gavest me. Wherefore, I cry unto Thee with the voice of the Prodigal: I have sinned before Thee, O compassionate Father. Receive me as one repentant, and make me as one of Thy hired servants.

MEAT-FARE SATURDAY

Troparion, Eighth Tone: O Thou Who by the depth of Thy wisdom, dost provide all things out of love for mankind, and grantest unto all that which is profitable, O only Creator: Grant rest, O Lord, to the souls of Thy servants, for in Thee have they placed their hope, O our Creator and Fashioner and God.

Kontakion, Eighth Tone: With the saints give rest, O Christ, to the souls of Thy servants, where there is neither sickness, nor sorrow, nor sighing, but life everlasting.

MEAT-FARE SUNDAY

Kontakion, First Tone: When Thou, O God, shalt come to earth with glory, and all things tremble, and the river of fire floweth before the Judgment Seat and the books are opened, and the hidden things made public, then deliver me from the unquenchable fire and deem me worthy to stand at Thy right hand, O most righteous Judge.

CHEESE-FARE SATURDAY

Troparion, Fourth Tone: O God of our fathers, Who ever dealest with us according to Thy kindness, take not Thy mercy from us, but through their intercessions guide our life in peace.

Kontakion, Eighth Tone: Thou hast made the assembly of the God-bearers illustrious as preachers of piety and silencers of ungodliness, O Lord, and they shine upon the world. By their supplications keep in perfect peace them that glorify and magnify Thee, that they may chant and sing unto Thee: Alleluia.

CHEESE-FARE SUNDAY

Kontakion, Sixth Tone: O Thou guide unto wisdom, bestower of prudence, instructor of the foolish and defender of the poor: Establish and grant understanding unto my heart, O Master. Grant me speech, O Word of the Father; for behold, I shall not keep my lips from crying unto Thee: O Merciful One, have mercy on me who have fallen.

The Prayer of St. Ephraim the Syrian:

O Lord and Master of my life, a spirit of idleness, despondency, ambition, and idle talking give me not. *Prostration.*

But rather a spirit of chastity, humble-mindedness, patience, and love bestow upon me Thy servant. *Prostration.*

Yea, O Lord King, grant me to see my failings and not condemn my brother; for blessed art Thou unto the ages of ages. Amen. *Prostration.*

O God, cleanse me a sinner, *(twelve times, with a reverence each time, and then repeat the entire prayer:)*

O Lord and Master of my life.... *and the rest, with a prostration at the end.*

[Note: This prayer is read at the hours of Wednesday and Friday of Cheese-Fare Week and in all of the Holy Great Lent, except on Saturdays and Sundays.]

THE FIRST WEEK OF GREAT LENT

Kontakion of the Great Canon, Sixth Tone: My soul, my soul, arise! Why sleepest thou? The end draweth nigh, and thou shalt be confounded; arouse thyself, then, that Christ God may spare thee, Who is everywhere present and filleth all things.

FIRST SATURDAY OF GREAT LENT

Troparion, Second Tone: Great are the achievements of faith! In the fountain of flame as in refreshing water, the holy martyr Theodore rejoiced; for having been made a whole-burnt offering in the fire, he was offered as sweet bread unto the Trinity. By his prayers, O Christ God, save our souls.

Kontakion, Eighth Tone: Having received the Faith of Christ in thy heart as a breastplate, thou didst trample upon the enemy hosts, O great champion; and thou hast been crowned eternally with a heavenly crown, as thou art invincible.

FIRST SUNDAY OF GREAT LENT

Troparion, Second Tone: We worship Thine immaculate Icon, O Good One, asking the forgiveness of our failings, O Christ God; for of Thine Own will Thou wast well-pleased to ascend the Cross in the flesh, that Thou mightest deliver from slavery to the enemy those whom Thou hadst fashioned. Wherefore, we cry to Thee thankfully: Thou didst fill all things with joy, O our Saviour, when Thou camest to save the world.

Kontakion, Eighth Tone: The Uncircumscribable Word of the Father was circumscribed when He took flesh of thee, O Theotokos; and when He had restored the defiled image to its ancient state, He suffused it with divine beauty. As for us, confessing our salvation, we record it in deed and word.

THE SECOND SUNDAY
OF GREAT LENT

Troparion, Eighth Tone: Light of Orthodoxy, pillar and teacher of the Church, adornment of monastics, invincible champion of theologians, O Gregory, thou wonderworker, boast of Thessalonica, herald of grace, ever pray that our souls be saved.

Kontakion, Eighth Tone: O sacred and divine organ of wisdom, clear trumpet of theology: we praise thee with one accord, O Gregory of divine speech; but as a mind standing before the Primordial Mind, direct our mind to Him, O father, that we may cry: Rejoice, O herald of grace!

Kontakion of the Sunday, Fourth Tone: The season of the virtues hath now been revealed, and judgment is at the doors; therefore let us arise and keep the Fast, offering tears of compunction together with our alms, and let us cry: Our sins are more than the sands of the sea; but do Thou pardon us, O Creator of all, that we may receive incorruptible crowns.

THE THIRD SUNDAY
OF GREAT LENT
The Veneration of the Cross

Troparion, First Tone: Save, O Lord, Thy people, and bless Thine inheritance; grant Thou unto Orthodox Christians victory over enemies; and by the power of Thy Cross do Thou preserve Thy commonwealth.

Kontakion, Fourth Tone: O Thou Who wast lifted up willingly on the Cross, bestow Thy mercies upon the new community named after Thee, O Christ God; gladden with Thy power the Orthdox Christians, granting them victory over enemies; may they have as Thy help the weapon of peace, the invincible trophy.

Another Kontakion, Seventh Tone: No longer doth the flaming sword guard the gate of Eden, for a strange extinction hath come upon it, even the Tree of the Cross. The sting hath been taken from death, and the victory from hades. And Thou, my Saviour, didst appear unto those in hades, saying: Enter ye again into Paradise.

THE FOURTH SUNDAY OF GREAT LENT
Saint John of the Ladder

Troparion, Third Tone: Having raised up a sacred ladder by thy words, thou wast shown forth unto all as a teacher of monastics, and thou dost lead us, O John, from the purification that cometh through godly discipline unto the light of divine vision. O righteous father, do thou entreat Christ God that we be granted great mercy.

Kontakion, First Tone: Offering teachings from thy book as ever-blossoming fruits, O wise one, thou dost sweeten the hearts of them that attend to them with vigilance, O blessed one; for it is a ladder that, from earth unto the heavenly and abiding glory, doth lead the souls of those who with faith do honour thee.

THE FIFTH SATURDAY
OF GREAT LENT
The Laudation of the Theotokos

Troparion, Eighth Tone: When the bodiless one learned the secret command, in haste he came and stood before Joseph's dwelling, and spake unto the Maiden who knew not wedlock: The One Who hath bowed the heavens by His descent is held and contained, unchanging, wholly in thee. Seeing Him receiving the form of a servant in thy womb, I stand in awe and cry to thee: Rejoice, thou Bride Unwedded!

Kontakion, Eighth Tone: To thee, the champion leader, we thy servants dedicate a feast of victory and of thanksgiving, as ones rescued out of sufferings, O Theotokos; but as thou art one with might which is invincible, from all dangers that can be do thou deliver us, that we may cry to thee: Rejoice, thou Bride Unwedded!

THE FIFTH SUNDAY OF GREAT LENT
Saint Mary of Egypt

Troparion, Fifth Tone: Enlightened by the grace of the Cross, thou wast shown forth as a radiant lamp of repentance, dispelling the darkness of the passions, O all-holy one. Wherefore, thou didst appear as an angel in the flesh unto the sacred Zosimas in the wilderness, O Mary, our righteous mother, do thou intercede with Christ for us.

Kontakion, Third Tone: Thou who once of old wast filled with all manner of fornication, art now seen today to be a bride of Christ by thy repentance. Thou didst love and emulate the life of the angels. By the Cross thou didst annihilate the hordes of demons; for this cause thou art a bride now in the kingdom of the heavens, O Mary, thou all-modest one.

Another Kontakion, Fourth Tone: Having escaped the darkness of sin, and having illumined thy heart with the light of repentance, O glorious one, thou didst come to Christ and didst offer to Him His immaculate and holy Mother as a merciful intercessor. Hence, thou hast found remission of thy transgressions, and thou ever rejoicest with the angels.

LAZARUS SATURDAY

Troparion, First Tone: In confirming the common Resurrection, O Christ God, Thou didst raise up Lazarus from the dead before Thy Passion. Wherefore, we also, like the children bearing the symbols of victory, cry to Thee, the Vanquisher of death: Hosanna in the highest; blessed is He that cometh in the name of the Lord.

Kontakion, Second Tone: Christ, the Joy of all, the Truth, the Light, the Life, the Resurrection of the world, hath, of His goodness, appeared to those on earth and become the archetype of the Resurrection, granting divine forgiveness unto all.

THE ENTRY OF THE LORD INTO JERUSALEM, PALM SUNDAY

Troparion, First Tone: In confirming the common Resurrection... *[See the Troparion for Lazarus Saturday].*

Another Troparion, Fourth Tone:
As by baptism we were buried with Thee, O Christ our God, so by Thy Resurrection we were deemed worthy of immortal life; and praising Thee, we cry: Hosanna in the highest; blessed is He that cometh in the name of the Lord.

Kontakion, Sixth Tone: Being borne upon a throne in heaven, and upon a colt on the earth, O Christ God, Thou didst accept the praise of the angels and the laudation of the children as they cry to Thee: Blessed is He that cometh to recall Adam.

PASSION WEEK TROPARIA
HOLY AND GREAT MONDAY
At Matins:

Troparion, Eighth Tone: Behold, the Bridegroom cometh at midnight, and blessed is that servant whom He shall find watching; but unworthy is he whom He shall find heedless. Beware, therefore, O my soul, lest thou be weighed down with sleep; lest thou be given up to death, and be shut out from the kingdom. But rouse thyself and cry: Holy, Holy, Holy art Thou, O God; through the Theotokos, have mercy on us. *Thrice.*

Kontakion, Eighth Tone:

Jacob lamented the loss of Joseph, but

that noble one was seated in a chariot and honoured as a king; for by not being enslaved then to the pleasures of the Egyptian woman, he was glorified by Him that beholdeth the hearts of men, and that bestoweth an incorruptible crown.

HOLY AND GREAT TUESDAY
At Matins:

Troparion, Eighth Tone: Behold, the Bridegroom cometh... *[See Monday, above].*

Kontakion, Second Tone:

Having realized the hour of the end, O my soul, and having feared at the cutting down of the fig tree, labour with the talent that was given thee, O hapless one, and be watchful and cry: Let us not remain outside the bridal-chamber of Christ.

HOLY AND GREAT WEDNESDAY
At Matins:

Troparion, Eighth Tone: Behold, the Bridegroom cometh... *[See Monday].*

Kontakion, Second Tone: Having transgressed more than the harlot, O Good One, I have in no wise brought forth streams of tears for Thee; but in silence I supplicate Thee and fall down before Thee, kissing Thine immaculate feet with love, so that, as Master that Thou art, Thou mayest grant me the forgiveness of debts, as I cry to Thee, O Saviour: From the mire of my deeds do Thou deliver me.

HOLY AND GREAT THURSDAY
At Matins:

Troparion, Eighth Tone: When the glorious disciples were enlightened at the washing of the feet, then Judas the ungodly one was stricken and darkened with the love of silver. And unto the lawless judges did he deliver Thee, the righteous Judge. Behold, O lover of money, him that for the sake thereof did hang himself; flee from that insatiable soul that dared such things against the Master. O Thou Who art good unto all, Lord, glory be to Thee.

Kontakion, Second Tone: Taking the bread into his hands, the betrayer stretcheth them forth secretly and receiveth the price of Him that, with His Own hands, fashioned, man. And Judas, the servant and deceiver, remained incorrigible.

HOLY AND GREAT FRIDAY

Troparion, Eighth Tone: When the glorious disciples... *[See Thursday]*.

Kontakion, Eighth Tone: Come, let us all praise Him Who was crucified for us, for Mary beheld Him on the Tree, and said: Though Thou endurest the Cross, Thou art my Son and my God.

HOLY AND GREAT SATURDAY

At Vespers and Saturday Matins:

Troparia, Second Tone: The noble Joseph, having taken Thy most pure Body down from the Tree and wrapped It in pure linen and covered It with spices, laid It in a new tomb.

When Thou didst descend unto death, O Life Immortal, then didst Thou slay hades with the lightning of Thy divinity. And when Thou didst also raise the dead out of the nethermost depths, all the Hosts of the heavens cried out: O Life-giver, Christ our God, glory be to Thee.

Unto the Myrrh-bearing Women did the angel cry out as he stood by the grave: Myrrh is meet for the dead, but Christ hath proved a stranger to corruption.

Kontakion, Second Tone: He that shut up the abyss is seen as one dead, and like a mortal, the Immortal One is wrapped in linen and myrrh, and placed in a grave. And women came to anoint Him, weeping bitterly and crying out: This is the most blessed Sabbath day wherein Christ, having slept, shall arise on the third day.

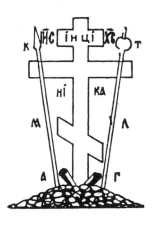

PASCHA

PROCESSIONAL HYMN

Sixth (Sticheron) Tone:

Thy Resurrection, O Christ Saviour, the angels hymn in the heavens; vouchsafe also us on earth with pure hearts to glorify Thee.

Paschal Troparion:

Christ is risen from the dead, trampling down death by death, and on those in the tombs bestowing life.

The Paschal Canon, First Tone:
ODE I

Eirmos: It is the Day of Resurrection, let us be radiant, O ye people; Pascha, the Lord's Pascha: for from death to life, and from earth to heaven, Christ God hath brought us, as we sing the hymn of victory.

Refrain: Christ is risen from the dead.

Let us purify our senses, and we shall behold Christ, radiant with the unapproachable light of the Resurrection, and we shall hear Him say, Rejoice!, as we sing the hymn of victory.

Let the heavens be glad as is meet, and let the earth rejoice, and let the whole world both visible and invisible, keep festival: for Christ is risen, O gladness eternal.

Katavasia: It is the Day of Resurrection....

ODE III

Eirmos: Come, let us drink a new drink, not one miraculously brought forth from a barren rock, but the Fountain of Incorruption, springing forth from the tomb of Christ, in Whom we are strengthened.

Refrain: Christ is risen from the dead.

Now all things are filled with light; heaven and earth, and the nethermost parts of the earth; let all creation, therefore, celebrate the arising of Christ, whereby it is strengthened.

Yesterday I was buried with Thee, O Christ; today I rise with Thine arising. Yesterday I was crucified with Thee; do Thou Thyself glorify me with Thee, O Saviour, in Thy kingdom.

Katavasia: Come, let us drink....

The Hypakoe, Eighth Tone:

Forestalling the dawn, the women came with Mary, and found the stone rolled away from the sepulchre, and heard from the angel: Why seek ye among the dead, as though He were mortal, Him Who liveth in everlasting light? Behold the grave-clothes. Go quickly and proclaim to the world that the Lord is risen and hath slain death. For He is the Son of God Who saveth mankind.

ODE IV

Eirmos: On divine watch let the God-inspired Abbachum stand with us, and show forth the light-bearing angel clearly saying: Today salvation is come to the world, for Christ is risen as Almighty.

Refrain: Christ is risen from the dead.

As a man-child did Christ appear when He came forth from the Virgin's womb, and as a mortal was He called the Lamb. Without blemish also, for He tasted no defilement, is our Pascha; and as true God, perfect was He proclaimed.

Like unto a yearling lamb, Christ, our blessed Crown, of His own will was sacrificed for all, a Pascha of purification; and from the tomb the beautiful Sun of Righteousness shone forth again upon us.

David, the ancestor of God, danced with leaping before the symbolical Ark; let us also, the holy people of God, beholding the fulfillment of the symbols, be divinely glad; for Christ is risen as Almighty.

Katavasia: On divine watch....

ODE V

Eirmos: Let us awake in the deep dawn, and instead of myrrh, offer a hymn to the Master, and we shall see Christ, the Sun of Righteousness, Who causeth life to dawn for all.

Refrain: Christ is risen from the dead.

Seeing Thy boundless compassion, they who were held in the bonds of hades hastened to the light, O Christ, with gladsome feet, praising the Pascha eternal.

Bearing lights, let us approach Christ, Who cometh forth from the tomb like a bridegroom, and with the feast-loving ranks of angels, let us celebrate the saving Pascha of God.

Katavasia: Let us awake....

ODE VI

Eirmos: Thou didst descend into the nethermost parts of the earth, and didst shatter the eternal bars that held the fettered, O Christ, and on the third day, like Jonah from the whale, Thou didst arise from the tomb.

Refrain: Christ is risen from the dead.

Having kept the seals intact, O Christ, Thou didst rise from the tomb, O Thou Who didst not break the seal of the Virgin by Thy birth, and Thou hast opened for us the doors of Paradise.

O my Saviour, the living and unslain Sacrifice, when as God, Thou, of Thine Own will, hadst offered up Thyself unto the Father, Thou didst raise up with Thyself the whole race of Adam, when Thou didst rise from the tomb.

Katavasia: Thou didst descend....

Kontakion, Eighth Tone:

Though Thou didst descend into the grave, O Immortal One, yet didst Thou destroy the power of hades. And didst arise as victor, O Christ God, calling to the myrrh-bearing women: Rejoice! and giving peace unto Thine apostles: Thou Who dost grant resurrection to the fallen.

Ekos:

The myrrh-bearing maidens forestalled the dawn, seeking, as it were day, the Sun that was before the sun and Who had once set in the tomb, and they cried out one to another: O friends! come, let us anoint with spices the life-bringing and buried Body, the Flesh that raised up fallen Adam, that now lieth in the tomb. Let us go, let us hasten, like the Magi, and let us worship and offer myrrh as a gift to Him Who is wrapped now not in swaddling clothes but in a shroud. And let us weep and cry aloud: O Master, arise, Thou Who dost grant resurrection to the fallen.

Then we chant:

Having beheld the Resurrection of Christ, let us worship the holy Lord Jesus, the only Sinless One. We worship Thy Cross, O Christ, and Thy holy Resurrection we hymn and glorify; for Thou art our God, and we know none other beside Thee, we call upon Thy name. O come, all ye faithful, let us worship Christ's holy Resurrection, for behold, through the Cross joy hath come to all the world. Ever blessing the Lord, we hymn His Resurrection; for, having endured crucifixion, He hath destroyed death by death. *Thrice.*

Jesus, having risen from the grave as He foretold, hath given us life eternal and great mercy. *Thrice.*

ODE VII

Eirmos: He Who delivered the Children from the furnace, became man, suffereth as a mortal, and through His Passion doth clothe mortality with the beauty of incorruption. He is the only blessed and most glorious God of our fathers.

Refrain: Christ is risen from the dead.

The godly-wise women with myrrh followed after Thee in haste; but Him Whom they sought with tears as dead, they worshipped joyfully as the living God, and they brought unto Thy disciples, O Christ, the good tidings of the mystical Pascha.

We celebrate the death of death, the destruction of hades, the beginning of another life eternal, and leaping for joy, we hymn the Cause, the only blessed and most glorious God of our fathers.

For truly sacred and all-festive is this saving night, and this shining, light-bearing day, the harbinger of the Resurrection, whereon the Timeless Light bodily from the tomb upon all hath shined.

ODE VIII

Eirmos: This is the chosen and holy day, the one king and lord of sabbaths, the feast of feasts, and the triumph of triumphs, on which we bless Christ unto the ages.

Refrain: Christ is risen from the dead.

Come, on this auspicious day of the Resurrection, let us partake of the fruit of the new vine of divine gladness of the kingdom of Christ, praising Him as God unto the ages.

Lift up thine eyes about thee, O Sion, and see, for behold, there cometh unto thee like God-illumined beacons, from the west, and from the north, and from the sea, and from the east, thy children, in thee blessing Christ unto the ages.

Refrain: O Most Holy Trinity, our God, glory to Thee.

O Father Almighty, and Word, and Spirit, one Nature united in three Persons, transcendent and most divine! Into Thee have we been baptized, and Thee will we bless unto all ages.

ODE IX

Refrain: Magnify, O my soul, Christ the Giver of life, Who rose from the grave on the third day.

Eirmos: Shine, shine, O new Jerusalem, for the glory of the Lord is risen upon thee; dance now and be glad, O Sion, and do thou exult, O pure Theotokos, in the arising of Him Whom thou didst bear.

Refrain: Magnify, O my soul, Him Who willingly suffered, and was buried, and rose from the grave on the third day.

Shine, shine,....

Refrain: Christ is the new Pascha, the living Sacrifice, the Lamb of God that taketh away the sin of the world.

Shine, shine,....

Refrain: The angel cried unto her that is full of grace: O pure Virgin, rejoice! and again I say, Rejoice! for thy Son is risen from the grave on the third day, and hath raised the dead, O ye people, be joyful!

Shine, shine,....

Refrain: Having slept, Thou didst awake the dead of the ages, roaring royally as the Lion of Judah.

O how divine, how loving, how sweet is Thy voice! For Thou hast truly promised to be with us unto the end of the age, O Christ; having this foundation of hope, we faithful rejoice.

Refrain: Mary Magdalene ran to the sepulchre, and having seen Christ, she questioned Him as though He were the gardener.

O how divine, how loving,...*repeat.*

Refrain: The shining angel to the women cried: Cease from tears, for Christ is risen.

O how divine, how loving,...*repeat.*

Refrain: Christ is risen, trampling down death, and raising the dead, O ye people, be joyful.

O how divine, how loving,...*repeat.*

Refrain: Today all creation is glad and rejoiceth, for Christ is risen, and hades is led in captivity.

O great and most sacred Pascha, Christ! O Wisdom and Word of God and Power! Grant us more perfectly to partake of Thee, in the unwaning day of Thy kingdom.

Refrain: Today the Master hath led hades captive, and raised the fettered, whom from ages it had held in bitter bondage.

O great and most sacred Pascha,....

Refrain: Magnify, O my soul, the dominion of the Tri-hypostatic and Indivisible Godhead.

O great and most sacred Pascha,....

Refrain: Rejoice, O Virgin, rejoice; rejoice, O blessed one; rejoice, O most glorified one: for thy Son is risen on the third day from the grave.

O great and most sacred Pascha,....

Refrain: Magnify, O my soul, Christ the Giver of life, Who rose from the grave on the third day.

Katavasia: Shine, shine,....

Exaposteilarion, Third Tone:

Having fallen asleep in the flesh, as a mortal, O King and Lord, on the third day Thou didst rise again, raising up Adam from corruption, and abolishing death: O Pascha of incorruption, salvation of the world! *Thrice.*

At LAUDS, in the First Tone:

Stichos: Praise Him for His mighty acts, praise Him according to the multitude of His greatness.

We hymn, O Christ, Thy saving Passion, and glorify Thy Resurrection.

Stichos: Praise Him with the sound of trumpet, praise Him with psaltery and harp.

O Thou Who didst endure the Cross, and didst abolish death, and didst rise again from the dead: Make our life peaceful, O Lord, for Thou alone art almighty.

Stichos: Praise Him with timbrel and dance, praise Him with strings and flute.

O Thou Who didst lead hades captive, and didst raise up man by Thy Resurrection, deem us worthy, with pure hearts, to hymn and glorify Thee.

Stichos: Praise Him with tuneful cymbals, praise Him with cymbals of jubilation. Let every breath praise the Lord.

Glorifying Thy Godly-majestic condescension, we hymn Thee, O Christ; for Thou wast born of a Virgin, yet Thou didst remain inseparable from the Father; Thou didst suffer as a man, and willingly didst endure the Cross; Thou didst rise from the tomb, coming forth as from a bridal chamber, that Thou mightest save the world: O Lord, glory be to Thee.

PASCHAL STICHERA, *Fifth Tone:*

Stichos: Let God arise and let His enemies be scattered.

A Pascha sacred today hath been shown unto us; a Pascha new and holy, a Pascha mystical, a Pascha all-venerable! A Pascha that is Christ the Redeemer; a Pascha immaculate, a great Pascha; a Pascha of the faithful; a Pascha that hath opened the gates of Paradise to us; a Pascha that doth sanctify all the faithful.

Stichos: As smoke vanisheth, so let them vanish.

Come from the vision, O ye women, bearers of good tidings, and say ye unto Sion: Receive from us the good tidings of the Resurrection of Christ; adorn thyself, exult, and rejoice, O Jerusalem, for thou hast seen Christ the King, like a bridegroom come forth from the tomb.

Stichos: So let sinners perish at the presence of God, and let the righteous be glad.

The myrrh-bearing women in the deep dawn stood before the tomb of the Giver of life; they found an angel sitting upon the stone, and he, speaking to them, said thus: Why seek ye the

Living among the dead? Why mourn ye the Incorruptible amid corruption? Go, proclaim unto His disciples.

Stichos: This is the day which the Lord hath made; let us rejoice and be glad therein.

Pascha the beautiful, Pascha, the Lord's Pascha, the Pascha all-venerable hath dawned upon us. Pascha, with joy let us embrace one another. O Pascha! ransom from sorrow, for from the tomb today, as from a bridal chamber, hath Christ shone forth, and hath filled the women with joy, saying: Proclaim unto the apostles.

Glory to the Father, and to the Son, and to the Holy Spirit, both now and ever, and unto the ages of ages. Amen.

It is the Day of Resurrection, let us be radiant for the feast, and let us embrace one another. Let us say, Brethren, even to them that hate us, let us forgive all things on the Resurrection, and thus let us cry out:

Christ is risen from the dead, trampling down death by death, and on those in the tombs bestowing life.

Then: Christ is risen from the dead, tramping down death by death, and on those in the tombs bestowing life! *Thrice.*

THE HOURS OF HOLY PASCHA

If there be a priest: Blessed is our God....

But a layman saith: Through the prayers of our holy fathers, O Lord Jesus Christ our God, have mercy on us. Amen.

Christ is risen from the dead, trampling down death by death, and on those in the tombs bestowing life. *Thrice. Then we chant thrice:*

Having beheld the Resurrection of Christ, let us worship the holy Lord Jesus, the only Sinless One. We worship Thy Cross, O Christ, and Thy holy Resurrection we hymn and glorify; for Thou art our God, and we know none other beside Thee, we call upon Thy name. O come, all ye faithful, let us worship Christ's holy Resurrection, for behold, through the Cross joy hath come to all the world. Ever blessing the Lord, we hymn His Resurrection; for, having endured crucifixion, He hath destroyed death by death. *Thrice.*

The Hypakoe, *Eighth Tone, once:*

Forestalling the dawn, the women came with Mary, and found the stone rolled away from the sepulchre, and heard from the angel: Why seek ye among the dead, as though He were mortal, Him Who liveth in everlasting light? Behold the grave-clothes. Go quickly and proclaim to the world that the Lord is risen and hath slain death. For He is the Son of God Who saveth mankind.

The Kontakion, *Eighth Tone, once:*

Though Thou didst descend into the grave, O Immortal One, yet didst Thou destroy the power of hades. And didst arise as victor, O Christ God, calling to the myrrh-bearing women: Rejoice! and giving peace unto Thine apostles: Thou Who dost grant resurrection to the fallen.

And these **Troparia,** *once:*

In the grave bodily, but in hades with Thy soul as God; in Paradise with the thief, and on the throne with the Father and the Spirit wast Thou Who fillest all things, O Christ the Inexpressible.

Glory to the Father, and to the Son, and to the Holy Spirit.

How life-giving, how much more beautiful than Paradise, and truly more resplendent than any royal palace was Thy tomb shown to be, O Christ, the source of our resurrection.

Both now and ever, and unto the ages of ages. Amen.

O sanctified and divine tabernacle of the Most High, rejoice! For through thee, O Theotokos, joy is given to them that cry: Blessed art thou among women, O all-spotless Lady.

Lord, have mercy. *Forty times.*

Glory to the Father, and to the Son,

and to the Holy Spirit, both now and ever, and unto the ages of ages. Amen.

More honourable than the Cherubim, and beyond compare more glorious than the Seraphim, who without corruption gavest birth to God the Word, the very Theotokos, thee do we magnify.

In the name of the Lord, Father (Master), bless.

Priest: Through the prayers of our holy fathers, O Lord Jesus Christ our God, have mercy on us.

And we say: Amen. *And we chant thrice:* Christ is risen.... Glory, both now.

Lord, have mercy. *Thrice.* Bless.

And the dismissal by the priest.

But a layman saith: O Lord Jesus Christ our God, for the sake of the intercessions of Thy most pure Mother, of our holy and God-bearing fathers, and all the saints, have mercy on us. Amen.

Troparia and Kontakia from the Pentecostarion

FRIDAY OF BRIGHT WEEK

The Life-giving Spring

Troparion, Third Tone: As a life-giving fount, thou didst conceive the Dew that is transcendent in essence, O Virgin Maid. And thou didst pour forth for us the Immortal Nectar. And as ever-flowing streams from thy fountain, thou broughtest forth the Water that springeth up unto life everlasting; wherein, taking delight, we all cry out: Rejoice, O life-bearing fount.

Kontakion, Eighth Tone: From thine unfailing fount, O Maiden full of grace, thou dost reward me by pouring forth of the unending streams of thy grace that passeth human understanding. And since thou didst bear the Word incomprehensibly, I entreat thee to refresh me with thy grace divine, that I may cry to thee: Rejoice, O water of salvation.

THOMAS SUNDAY

Troparion, Seventh Tone: While the tomb was sealed, Thou, O Life, didst shine forth from the grave, O Christ God. And while the doors were shut, Thou didst come unto Thy disciples, O Resurrection of all, renewing through them an upright Spirit in us according to Thy great mercy.

Kontakion, Eighth Tone: With his searching right hand, Thomas did probe Thy life-bestowing side, O Christ

God; for when Thou didst enter while the doors were shut, he cried out unto Thee with the rest of the disciples: Thou art my Lord and my God.

SUNDAY OF THE MYRRH-BEARING WOMEN

Troparion, Second Tone: When Thou didst descend unto death, O Life Immortal, then didst Thou slay hades with the lightning of Thy Divinity. And when Thou didst also raise the dead out of the nethermost depths, all the Hosts of the heavens cried out: O Life-giver, Christ our God, glory be to Thee.

The noble Joseph, taking Thine immaculate Body down from the Tree, and having wrapped It in pure linen and spices, laid It in a new tomb. But on the third day Thou didst arise, O Lord, granting to the world great mercy.

Unto the myrrh-bearing women did the angel cry out as he stood by the tomb: Myrrh is meet for the dead, but Christ hath proved to be a stranger to corruption. But cry out: The Lord is risen, granting to the world great mercy.

Kontakion, Second Tone: When Thou didst cry. Rejoice, unto the myrrh-bearers, Thou didst make the lamentation of Eve the first mother to cease by Thy Resurrection, O Christ God. And Thou didst bid Thine apostles to preach: The Saviour is risen from the grave.

SUNDAY OF THE PARALYTIC

Kontakion, Third Tone: As of old Thou didst raise the paralytic, O Lord, by Thy Divine presence, raise my soul, which is paralyzed grievously by all manner of sins and unseemly deeds, that being saved I may cry out: O compassionate Christ, glory be to Thy power.

MID-PENTECOST WEDNESDAY

Troparion, Eighth Tone: In the midst of the Feast, give Thou my thirsty soul to drink of the waters of piety; for Thou, O Saviour, didst cry out to all: Whosoever is thirsty, let him come to Me and drink. Wherefore, O Well-spring of life, Christ our God, glory be to Thee.

Kontakion, Fourth Tone: In the midst of the Judaic feast, Thou didst say to those present, O Christ God, Master and Creator of all: Come ye and receive the Water of immortality. Wherefore, we fall down before Thee, crying out in faith and saying: Grant us Thy mercy and compassion; for Thou art the Well-spring of our life.

SUNDAY OF
THE SAMARITAN WOMAN

Kontakion, Eighth Tone: Having come to the well in faith, the Samaritan woman saw Thee, the Water of Wisdom, whereof having drunk abundantly, she, the renowned one, inherited the kingdom on high forever.

SUNDAY OF THE BLIND MAN

Kontakion, Fourth Tone: Blinded in the eyes of my soul, I draw nigh unto Thee, O Christ, like the man blind from his birth, and in repentance I cry to Thee: Thou art the exceeding radiant Light of those in darkness.

THE ASCENSION OF THE LORD

Troparion, Fourth Tone: Thou hast ascended in glory, O Christ our God, having gladdened Thy disciples with the promise of the Holy Spirit; and they were assured by the blessing that Thou art the Son of God, the Redeemer of the world.

Kontakion, Sixth Tone: When Thou didst fulfill Thy dispensation for our sake, uniting things on earth with the heavens, Thou didst ascend in glory, O Christ our God, departing not hence, but remaining inseparable from us, and crying unto them that love Thee: I am with you, and no one shall be against you.

THE SUNDAY OF THE
HOLY FATHERS OF THE
FIRST ECUMENICAL COUNCIL

Troparion, Eighth Tone: Most glorified art Thou, O Christ our God, Who hast established our holy fathers as luminous stars upon the earth, and through them didst guide us all to the true Faith. O Most-merciful One, glory be to Thee.

Kontakion, Eighth Tone: The preaching of the apostles and the doctrines of the fathers confirmed the one Faith of the Church. And wearing the garment of truth, woven from the theology on high, She rightly divideth and glorifieth the great mystery of piety.

PENTECOST SUNDAY

Troparion, Eighth Tone: Blessed art Thou, O Christ our God, Who hast shown forth the fishermen as supremely wise, by sending down upon them the Holy Spirit, and through them didst draw the world into Thy net. O Lover of mankind, glory be to Thee. **Kontakion, Eighth Tone:** Once, when He descended and confounded the tongues, the Most High divided the nations; and when He divided the tongues of fire, He called all men into unity; and with one accord we glorify the All-Holy Spirit.

SUNDAY OF ALL SAINTS

Troparion, Fourth Tone: Adorned in the blood of Thy martyrs throughout all the world, as in purple and fine linen. Thy Church, through them doth cry unto Thee, O Christ God: Send down Thy compassions upon Thy people; grant peace to Thy flock and to our souls great mercy.

Kontakion, Eighth Tone: To Thee, the Planter of creation, the world doth offer the God-bearing martyrs as the firstfruits of nature. By their intercessions preserve Thy Church, Thy commonwealth, in profound peace, through the Theotokos, O Greatly-merciful One.

SECOND SUNDAY AFTER PENTECOST
ALL SAINTS OF RUSSIA

Troparion, Eighth Tone: As a beautiful fruit of the sowing of Thy salvation, the land of Russia doth offer to Thee, O Lord, all the saints that have shone in her. By their intercessions preserve the Church and our land in profound peace, through the Theotokos, O Greatly-merciful One.

Kontakion, Third Tone: Today the choir of the saints who pleased God in the land of Russia doth stand before us in church and invisibly doth pray for us to God. With them the angels glorify Him, and all the saints of the Church of Christ keep festival with them; and they all pray together for us to the Eternal God.

A SUPPLICATORY CANON
to our Lord Jesus Christ

Second Tone:

ODE I

Eirmos: In the deep of old the infinite Power overwhelmed Pharaoh's whole army. But the incarnate Word annihilated pernicious sin. Exceedingly glorious is the Lord, for gloriously is He glorified.

Refrain: O sweetest Jesus, save us.

Sweetest Jesus Christ, long-suffering Jesus, heal the wounds of my soul, Jesus, and make sweet my heart, O Greatly-merciful One, I pray Thee, Jesus my Saviour, that being saved by

Thee, I may magnify Thee.

O sweetest Jesus, save us.

Sweetest Jesus Christ, open to me the door of repentance, O Jesus, Lover of mankind, and accept me, O Jesus my Saviour, as I fall down before Thee and fervently implore the forgiveness of my sins.

O sweetest Jesus, save us.

O sweetest Jesus Christ, Jesus, snatch me from the hand of deceitful Belial, O Jesus, and make me stand at the right hand of Thy glory, O Jesus my Saviour, delivering me from the lot of those on the left.

O most holy Theotokos, save us.

Theotokion: O Lady who gavest birth to Jesus our God, pray for us worthless servants, that by thy prayers, O immaculate one, we who are defiled may be delivered from torment, O spotless one, and enjoy everlasting glory.

ODE III

Eirmos: By establishing me on the rock of faith, Thou hast enlarged my mouth over mine enemies, and my spirit rejoiceth when I sing: There is none holy as our God, and none righteous beside Thee, O Lord.

O sweetest Jesus, save us.

Hearken, O my Jesus, Lover of mankind, unto Thy servant calling with compunction; and deliver me, O Jesus, from condemnation and torment, O only long-suffering sweetest Jesus, plenteous in mercy.

O sweetest Jesus, save us.

Receive Thy servant, O my Jesus, who falleth down with tears, O my Jesus, and save me as one repentant, O my Jesus, delivering me from Gehenna, O Master, sweetest Jesus, plenteous in mercy.

O sweetest Jesus, save us.

O my Jesus, the time Thou gavest me I have squandered in passions, O my Jesus. Reject me not, O my Jesus, but call me, I pray, O Master, sweetest Jesus, and save me.

O most holy Theotokos, save us.

Theotokion: O Virgin who gavest birth to my Jesus, implore Him to deliver me from Gehenna. Thou alone art the protectress of the afflicted, O thou who art full of divine grace. And vouchsafe me the life that ageth not, O all-blameless one.

Lord, have mercy. *Thrice.*

Glory to the Father, and to the Son, and to the Holy Spirit, both now and ever, and unto the ages of ages. Amen.

Sedalen: O Jesus my Saviour, Thou didst save the prodigal. Jesus my Saviour, Thou didst accept the harlot. And now have mercy on me, O Jesus plenteous in mercy; have compassion and save me, O Jesus my Benefactor, as Thou hadst compassion on Manasseh, my Jesus, only Lover of mankind.

ODE IV

Eirmos: From a Virgin didst Thou come, not as an ambassador, nor as an angel, but the very Lord Himself incarnate, and didst save me, the whole man. Wherefore, I cry to Thee: Glory to Thy power, O Lord.

O sweetest Jesus, save us.

Heal, O my Jesus, the wounds of my soul, O my Jesus, I pray, and snatch me from the hand of soul-corrupting Belial, O my compassionate Jesus, and save me.

O sweetest Jesus, save us.

I have sinned, O my sweetest Jesus; O Compassionate One, O my Jesus, save me who flee to Thy protection, O long-suffering Jesus, and vouchsafe me Thy kingdom.

O sweetest Jesus, save us.

No one hath sinned, O my Jesus, as have I, the wretched one; but now I fall down praying: Save me, O my Jesus, and grant me life, O my Jesus.

O most holy Theotokos, save us.

Theotokion: O all-hymned one, who gavest birth to the Lord Jesus, implore Him to deliver from torment all who hymn thee and call thee truly the Theotokos.

ODE V

Eirmos: O Thou Who art the Light of those lying in darkness, and the salvation of the despairing, O Christ my Saviour, I rise early to pray to Thee, O King of Peace. Enlighten me with Thy radiance, for I know none other God beside Thee.

O sweetest Jesus, save us.

Thou art the light of my mind, O my Jesus; Thou art the salvation of my despairing soul, O Saviour. O my Jesus, do Thou deliver me from torment and Gehenna, as I cry: Save me, the wretched one, O Christ my Jesus.

O sweetest Jesus, save us.

Utterly cast down to shameful passions, O my Jesus, I now cry: Stretch down to me a helping hand, O my

Jesus, and pluck me out as I cry: Save me, the wretched one, O Christ my Jesus.

O sweetest Jesus, save us.

Carrying about a mind defiled, I call to Thee, O Jesus: Cleanse me from the dirt of sin, and redeem me who slipped down to the depths of evil through ignorance, and save me, O Saviour my Jesus, I pray.

O most holy Theotokos, save us.

Theotokion: O maiden Mother of God, who gavest birth to Jesus, implore Him to save all Orthodox monastics and laity, and to deliver from Gehenna those who cry: Beside thee we know no certain protection.

ODE VI

Eirmos: Whirled about in the abyss of sin, I appeal to the unfathomable abyss of Thy compassion: From corruption raise me up, O God.

O sweetest Jesus, save us.

O my Jesus Christ plenteous in

mercy, accept me who confess my sins, O Master, and save me, O Jesus, and snatch me from corruption, O Jesus.

O sweetest Jesus, save us.

O my Jesus, no one else hath been so prodigal as I, the wretched one, O Jesus, Lover of mankind, but do Thou Thyself save me, O Jesus.

O sweetest Jesus, save us.

O my Jesus, with my passions I have surpassed the harlot and the prodigal, Manasseh and the publican, O my Jesus, and the robber and the Ninevites, O Jesus.

O most holy Theotokos, save us.

Theotokion: O thou who didst give birth to my Jesus Christ, O only undefiled and immaculate Virgin, cleanse me now, the defiled one, by the hyssop of thine intercessions.

ODE VII

Eirmos: When the golden image was worshipped in the plain of Dura, Thy three children despised the godless order. Thrown into the fire, they were bedewed and sang: Blessed art Thou, O God of our fathers.

O sweetest Jesus, save us.

O Christ Jesus, no one on earth hath ever sinned, O my Jesus, as I, the wretched one and prodigal, have sinned. Wherefore, I cry to Thee, my Jesus, have compassion on me as I sing: Blessed art Thou, O God of our fathers.

O sweetest Jesus, save us.

O Christ Jesus, I cry: Nail me down with the fear of Thee, O my Jesus, and pilot me to Thy calm haven now, O my compassionate Jesus, that as one saved I may sing to Thee: Blessed art Thou, O God of our fathers.

O sweetest Jesus, save us.

O Christ Jesus, ten thousand times have I, the passionate one, promised Thee repentance, O my Jesus, but wretch that I am, I deceived Thee.

Wherefore, I cry to Thee, my Jesus:
Enlighten my soul which remaineth
unfeeling; O Christ, the God of our
fathers, blessed art Thou.

O most holy Theotokos, save us.

Theotokion: O thou who gavest
birth to Jesus awesomely and above
nature, O all-blameless one, implore
Him, O Maiden, to forgive me all the
sins that I have committed against my
nature, that as one saved I may cry:
Blessed art thou who didst give birth to
God in the flesh.

ODE VIII

Eirmos: O ye works, praise the Lord God,
Who descended into the fiery furnace with the
Hebrew children and changed the flame into
dew, and supremely exalt Him unto all ages.

O sweetest Jesus, save us.

I implore Thee, O my Jesus: As
Thou didst redeem the harlot from
many sins, O my Jesus, likewise redeem
me, O Christ my Jesus, and cleanse my

foul soul, O my Jesus.

O sweetest Jesus, save us.

O Jesus, having yielded to irrational pleasures, I have become irrational, O my Jesus; and wretch that I am, I have truly become like unto the beasts, O my Saviour. Wherefore, O Jesus, deliver me from irrationality.

O sweetest Jesus, save us.

Having fallen, O Jesus, into the hands of soul-corrupting thieves, I have been stripped now of my divinely-woven garment, O my Jesus, and I am lying all bruised with wounds. O my Christ, do Thou pour on me oil and wine.

O most holy Theotokos, save us.

Theotokion: O Theotokos Mary, who ineffably didst carry the Christ, my Jesus and God: Do thou ever implore Him to save from perils thy servants and them that praise thee, O Virgin who knewest not wedlock.

ODE IX

Eirmos: God the Word, Who came forth from God, and Who by ineffable wisdom came to renew Adam after his grievous fall to corruption through eating, and Who ineffably took flesh from the holy Virgin for our sake, Him do we the faithful with one accord magnify with hymns.

O sweetest Jesus, save us.

I have surpassed, O my Jesus, Manasseh and the publican, the harlot and the prodigal, O compassionate Jesus, and the robber, O my Jesus, through all my shameful and unseemly deeds, O Jesus; but do Thou forestall me, O my Jesus, and save me.

O sweetest Jesus, save us.

By my passions, O my Jesus, have I, the wretched one, surpassed all those from Adam who have sinned both before the Law and in the Law, O Jesus, and after the Law and Grace, O my Jesus; but by Thy judgments save me, O my Jesus.

O sweetest Jesus, save us.

May I not be parted from Thine ineffable glory, my Jesus, nor may the portion on the left fall to me, O sweetest Jesus; but set me on the right hand with Thy sheep and give me rest, O Christ my Jesus, since Thou art compassionate.

O most holy Theotokos, save us.

Theotokion: O Theotokos, who didst carry Jesus, O only unwedded Virgin Mary who knewest not wedlock, O pure one, invoke Him, thy Son and Creator, to deliver them that hasten to thee from temptation and perils, and the fire that is to come.

Prayer to Our Lord Jesus Christ

O Lord and Master, Jesus Christ my God, Who, for the sake of Thine ineffable love for mankind, at the end of the ages wast wrapped in flesh from the Ever-Virgin Mary, I glorify Thy saving providence and care for me, Thy servant, O Master. I praise Thee, for through Thee I have learned to know the Father; I bless Thee through Whom the Holy Spirit came into the world; I bow to Thy most pure Mother who served for the dread mystery of Thine incarnation; I praise the angelic choir as the servants and singers of Thy majesty; I bless Saint John the Forerunner who baptized Thee, O Lord; I honour also the prophets who announced Thee, I glorify Thy holy apostles; I celebrate the martyrs, I glorify Thy priests; I venerate Thy saints and praise all Thy righteous ones. This such countless and unutterable divine choir I, Thy servant, in prayer offer to Thee, O All-compassionate God, and therefore I ask the forgiveness of my sins, which do Thou grant me for the sake of all Thy saints, but especially for the sake of Thy holy compassion, for blessed art Thou unto the ages. Amen.

SUPPLICATORY CANON
To the Most Holy Theotokos

Troparion, Fourth Tone: To the Theotokos let us run now most earnestly, we sinners all and wretched ones, and fall down, in repentance calling from the depths of our souls: O Lady, come unto our aid, have compassion upon us; hasten thou, for we are lost in a throng of transgressions. Turn not thy servants away with empty hands, for thee alone do we have as our only hope. *Twice.*

Glory to the Father, and to the Son, and to

the Holy Spirit, both now and ever, and unto the ages of ages. Amen.

Never, O Theotokos, will we cease to speak of thy powers, unworthy as we are. For if thou didst not intercede in prayer, who would have delivered us from so many dangers? Who would have kept us free until now? Let us never forsake thee, O Lady, for thou dost ever save thy servants from all perils.

Canon, Eighth Tone:
ODE I

Eirmos: Having passed through the water as on dry land, and having escaped the malice of the Egyptians, the Israelites cried aloud: Unto our God and Redeemer let us now sing.

Refrain: O most holy Theotokos, save us.

Distressed by many temptations, I flee to thee, seeking salvation. O Mother of the Word, and Virgin, from ordeals and afflictions deliver me.

O most holy Theotokos, save us.

Outbursts of passions trouble me and fill my soul with great despondency. Calm it, O Maiden, by the peace of thy Son and God, O all-blameless one.

Glory to the Father, and to the Son, and to the Holy Spirit.

I implore thee who gavest birth to the Saviour and God, O Virgin to deliver me from perils. For, fleeing now unto thee for refuge, I lift up both my soul and my reasoning.

Both now and ever, and unto the ages of ages. Amen.

Ailing am I in body and soul, do thou vouchsafe me the divine visitation, and thy care, O thou who alone art the Mother of God, for thou art good and the Mother of the Good.

ODE III

Eirmos: Of the vault of the heavens art Thou, O Lord, the Maker, and Builder of the Church; do Thou establish in me love of Thee, O Summit of desire, O Support of the faithful, O only Lover of mankind.

O most holy Theotokos, save us.

I have chosen thee to be the protection and intercession of my life, O Virgin, Mother of God. Pilot me to thy haven, O author of blessings, O support of the faithful, O thou only all-lauded one.

O most holy Theotokos, save us.

I pray thee, O Virgin, to dispel the tumult of my soul and the storm of my grief; for thou, O Bride of God, hast given birth to Christ, the Prince of Peace, O only immaculate one.

Glory to the Father, and to the Son, and to the Holy Spirit.

Since thou broughtest forth Him Who is the Benefactor and Cause of good, from the wealth of thy loving-kindness do thou pour forth on all; for thou canst do all things, since thou didst bear Christ, the One Who is mighty in power; for blessed of God art thou.

Both now and ever, and unto the ages of ages. Amen.

I am tortured by grievous sicknesses and morbid passions: O Virgin, do thou help me; for I know thee to be an inexhaustible treasury of unfailing healing, O all-blameless one.

Lord have mercy. *Thrice.*

Glory to the Father, and to the Son, and to the Holy Spirit, both now and ever, and unto the ages of ages. Amen.

Sessional Hymn, Second Tone:

O fervent advocate, invincible battlement, fountain of mercy, and sheltering retreat for the world, earnestly we cry to thee: O Lady Theotokos, hasten thou, and save us from all imperilment; for thou alone art our speedy protectress.

ODE IV

Eirmos: I have heard, O Lord, of the mystery of Thy dispensation, and I came to knowledge of Thy works, and glorify Thy Divinity.

O most holy Theotokos, save us.

The turmoil of my passions, and the storm of my sins do thou bestill, thou who gavest birth to the Lord and Pilot, O thou Bride of God.

O most holy Theotokos, save us.

O bestow, out of the abyss of thy compassion, on me thy supplicant; for thou didst give birth to the Kind-hearted One and Saviour of all that hymn thee.

O most holy Theotokos, save us.

While delighting in thy gifts, O spot-less one, we sing a song of thanksgiving to thee, knowing thee to be the Mother of God.

Glory to the Father, and to the Son, and to the Holy Spirit.

As I lie on the bed of my pain and infirmity, do thou help me, as thou art a lover of goodness, O Theotokos, who alone art Ever-Virgin.

Both now and ever, and unto the ages of ages. Amen.

Having thee as our staff and hope, and as our salvation's unshaken battlement, from all manner of adversity are we then redeemed, O thou all-lauded one.

ODE V

Eirmos: Enlighten us by Thy commands, O Lord, and by Thy lofty arm bestow Thy peace upon us, O Lover of mankind.

O most holy Theotokos, save us.

Fill my heart with gladness, O pure one, by giving me thine incorruptible joy, O thou who didst bear the Cause of gladness.

O most holy Theotokos, save us.

Deliver us from dangers, O pure Theotokos, who didst give birth to Eternal Redemption, and the Peace that doth pass all understanding.

Glory to the Father, and to the Son, and to the Holy Spirit.

Dispel the darkness of my sins, O Bride of God, by the radiance of thy splendour, for thou didst bear the Light Divine and Pre-eternal.

Both now and ever, and unto the ages of ages. Amen.

Heal, O pure one, the infirmity of my soul, when thou hast deemed me worthy of thy visitation, and grant me health by thine intercessions.

ODE VI

Eirmos: I will pour out my prayer unto the Lord, and to Him will I proclaim my grief; for with evils my soul is filled, and my life unto hades hath drawn nigh, and like Jonah I will pray: From corruption raise me up, O God.

O most holy Theotokos, save us.

My nature, held by corruption and death, hath He saved from out of death and corruption; for unto death He Himself hath submitted. Wherefore, O Virgin, do thou intercede with Him Who is thy Lord and Son, to deliver me from enemies' wickedness.

O most holy Theotokos, save us.

I know thee as the protection of my

life, and most safe fortification, O Virgin; disperse the horde of temptations, and drive away demonic vexation; unceasingly I pray to thee: From corruption of passions deliver me.

Glory to the Father, and to the Son, and to the Holy Spirit.

We have acquired thee as a wall of refuge, and the perfect salvation of our souls, and a relief in afflictions, O Maiden, and we ever rejoice in thy light. O Sovereign Lady, do thou also now save us from passions and dangers.

Both now and ever, and unto the ages of ages. Amen.

Bedridden, I lie supine with sickness now, and there is no healing for my flesh; but to thee, O good one who gavest birth to God and the Saviour of the world and the Healer of infirmities, I pray: From corruption of illness raise me up.

Kontakion, Sixth Tone:

O protection of Christians that cannot be put to shame, O mediation unto the Creator unfailing: Disdain not the suppliant voices of sinners; but be thou quick, O good one, to help us who in faith cry unto thee: hasten to intercession, and speed thou to make supplication, thou who dost ever protect, O Theotokos, them that honour thee.

Sticheron, same tone:

Entrust me not to human protection, O most holy Lady, but receive the supplication of thy servant; for sorrow hath fettered me, I cannot endure the demon's darts; a shelter have I not, neither place to run, I the wretched one; always I am fleeing and no consolation have I but thee, O Sovereign Lady of creation, hope and protection of the faithful; turn not away from my supplication, do that which will profit me.

ODE VII

Eirmos: Having gone down to Babylon from Judea, the Children of old by their faith in the Trinity trod down the flame of the furnace while chanting: O God of the fathers, blessed art Thou.

O most holy Theotokos, save us.

Having willed to accomplish our salvation, O Saviour, Thou didst dwell in the womb of the Virgin, and didst show her to the world as the mediatress; O God of our fathers, blessed art Thou.

O most holy Theotokos, save us.

The Dispenser of mercy, Whom thou didst bear, O pure Mother, do thou implore to deliver from transgressions and defilements of the soul, those who with faith cry out: O God of our fathers, blessed art Thou.

Glory to the Father, and to the Son, and to the Holy Spirit.

A treasury of salvation, and a fountain of incorruption is she who gave Thee birth; a tower of safety, and a door of repentance hast Thou proved her to them that shout: O God of our fathers, blessed art Thou.

Both now and ever, and unto the ages of ages. Amen.

For weakness of body and sickness of soul, O Theotokos, do thou vouchsafe healing to those who with love draw near to thy protection, O Virgin, who for us gavest birth to Christ the Saviour.

ODE VIII

Eirmos: The King of Heaven, Whom hosts of angels hymn, praise ye and supremely exalt unto all ages.

O most holy Theotokos, save us.

Disdain not those who need thy help, O Virgin, and who hymn and supremely exalt thee unto the ages.

O most holy Theotokos, save us.

Thou healest the infirmity of my soul and the pains of my body, O Virgin, that I may glorify thee, O pure one, unto the ages.

Glory to the Father, and to the Son, and to the Holy Spirit.

Thou pourest forth a wealth of healing, on those who with faith hymn thee, O Virgin, and who supremely exalt thine ineffable Offspring.

Both now and ever, and unto the ages of ages. Amen.

Thou drivest away the assaults of temptations, and the attacks of the passions, O Virgin; wherefore do we hymn thee unto all ages.

ODE IX

Eirmos: Truly we confess thee to be the Theotokos, we who through thee have been saved, O pure Virgin; with the bodiless choirs, thee do we magnify.

O most holy Theotokos, save us.

Turn not away from the torrent of my tears, O Virgin, thou who didst give birth to Christ, Who doth wipe away all tears from every face.

O most holy Theotokos, save us.

Fill my heart with joy, O Virgin, thou who didst receive the fullness of joy, and didst banish the grief of sin.

O most holy Theotokos, save us.

Be the haven and protection, and a wall unshaken, a refuge and shelter, and the gladness, O Virgin, of those who flee unto thee.

Glory to the Father, and to the Son, and to the Holy Spirit.

Illumine with the rays of thy light, O Virgin, those who piously confess thee to be the Theotokos, and do thou banish away all darkness of ignorance.

Both now and ever, and unto the ages of ages. Amen.

Theotokion: In a place of affliction and infirmity am I brought low; O

Virgin, do thou heal me, transforming mine illness into healthfulness.

Prayer to the Most Holy Theotokos:
O my most blessed Queen, O Theotokos my hope, guardian of orphans, intercessor for strangers, joy of the sorrowful, protectress of the wronged: thou seest my misfortune, thou seest mine affliction; help me, for I am weak; feed me, for I am a stranger. Thou knowest mine offence: absolve it as thou wilt, for I have no other help beside thee, no other intercessor, nor good consoler, except thee, O Mother of God. Do thou preserve and protect me unto the ages of ages. Amen.

CANON
to the Guardian Angel

Troparion, Sixth Tone: O Angel of God, my holy guardian, keep my life in the fear of Christ God; strengthen my mind in the true way, and wound my soul with heavenly love, so that, guarded by thee, I may obtain of Christ God great mercy.

Glory to the Father, and to the Son, and to the Holy Spirit, both now and ever, and unto the ages of ages. Amen.

Theotokion: O holy Lady, Mother of Christ our God, thou didst inexplicably bear the Creator of all; with my guardian angel entreat always His goodness to save my soul, possessed by passions, and to grant me remission of sins.

Canon, Eighth Tone:

Eirmos: Let us sing to the Lord, Who led His people through the Red Sea, for He alone is gloriously glorified.

Refrain: O Lord Jesus Christ my God, have mercy on me.

To Jesus: Vouchsafe me, Thy servant, O Saviour, worthily to sing a song and to praise the fleshless angel, my guide and guardian.

Holy Angel of the Lord, my guardian, pray to God for me.

Alone I lie in folly and idleness, O my guide and guardian, forsake not me who am perishing.

Glory to the Father, and to the Son, and to the Holy Spirit.

Direct my mind by thy prayer to fulfill the commands of God, that I may obtain of God forgiveness of sins, and teach me to hate all wickedness, I pray thee.

Both now and ever, and unto the ages of ages. Amen.

With my guardian angel, O Virgin, pray for me, thy servant, to the Gracious One, and teach me to fulfill the commandments of thy Son and my Creator.

ODE III

Eirmos: Thou art the support of those who flee unto Thee, O Lord, Thou art the light of those in darkness, and my spirit doth hymn Thee.

Refrain: Holy Angel of the Lord, my guardian, pray to God for me.

All my thoughts and my soul I have committed unto thee, O my guardian; do thou deliver me from all attacks of the enemy.

Holy Angel of the Lord, my guardian, pray to God for me.

The enemy troubleth and trampleth on me, and teacheth me always to do his will, but do thou, O my guide, forsake not me who am perishing.

Glory to the Father, and to the Son, and to the Holy Spirit.

Grant me to sing a song with thanksgiving and fervour unto my Creator and God, and to thee, my good Angel Guardian; O my deliverer, rescue me from foes that do me evil.

Both now and ever, and unto the ages of ages. Amen.

Heal, O immaculate one, the most painful wounds of my soul, and drive away the enemies that ever fight against me.

Lord, have mercy. *Thrice.*

Sessional Hymn, Second Tone:

Out of the love of my soul I cry to thee, O guardian of my soul, mine all-holy Angel! Protect and guard me always from the hunting of the evil one, and guide me to the heavenly life, teaching and enlightening and strengthening me.

Glory to the Father, and to the Son, and to the Holy Spirit, both now and ever, and unto the ages of ages. Amen.

Theotokion: O Theotokos Unwedded, O most pure one who gavest birth without seed to the Master of all, together with my guardian angel entreat Him to deliver me from all perplexity, and to grant my soul compunction and light, and cleansing of sins, for thou alone art quick to help.

ODE IV

Eirmos: I have heard, O Lord, of the mystery of Thy dispensation, and I came to knowledge of Thy works, and I glorify Thy Divinity.

Refrain: Holy Angel of the Lord, my guardian, pray to God for me.

Pray thou to God, the Lover of mankind, and forsake me not, O my guardian, but ever keep my life in peace, and grant me the invincible salvation.

Holy Angel of the Lord, my guardian, pray to God for me.

As the defender and guardian of my life I received thee from God, O Angel. I pray thee, O holy one, free me from all danger.

Glory to the Father, and to the Son, and to the Holy Spirit.

Cleanse my defilement by thy holiness, O my guardian, and may I be drawn from the left side by thy prayers, and become a partaker of glory.

Both now and ever, and unto the ages of ages.

Perplexity confronteth me from the evil surrounding me, O most pure one, but deliver me from it speedily, for I flee only to thee.

ODE V

Eirmos: Awaking at dawn, we cry to Thee: O Lord, save us; for Thou art our God, beside Thee we know none other.

Refrain: Holy Angel of the Lord, my guardian, pray to God for me.

As one having boldness toward God, O my holy guardian, do thou entreat Him to deliver me from the evils that afflict me.

Holy Angel of the Lord, my guardian, pray

to God for me.

O radiant light, illumine my soul with radiance, O my guide and guardian, given me by God, O Angel.

Glory to the Father, and to the Son, and to the Holy Spirit.

Keep me vigilant who sleep from the evil burden of sin, O Angel of God, and raise me up to glorify Him, through thy supplication.

Both now and ever, and unto the ages of ages. Amen.

O Mary, Lady Theotokos unwedded, O hope of the faithful, subdue the uprisings of the enemy, and gladden them that hymn thee.

ODE VI

Eirmos: Grant me a garment of light, O Thou Who coverest Thyself with light as with a garment, O plenteously-merciful Christ our God.

Refrain: Holy Angel of the Lord, my guardian, pray to God for me.

Free me from every temptation, and

save me from sorrow, I pray thee, O holy Angel, given to me as my good guardian by God.

Holy Angel of the Lord, my guardian, pray to God for me.

Enlighten my mind, O good one, and illumine me, I pray thee, O holy Angel, and teach me to think always profitably.

Glory to the Father, and to the Son, and to the Holy Spirit.

Abolish present disturbance from my heart, and strengthen me to be vigilant in good, O my guardian, and guide me miraculously to quietness of life.

Both now and ever, and unto the ages of ages. Amen.

The Word of God dwelt in thee, O Theotokos, and showed thee to men as the heavenly ladder; for by thee the Most High descended to us.

Kontakion, Fourth Tone:

Show compassion to me, O holy

angel of the Lord, my guardian, and leave not me, a defiled one, but illumine me with the light unapproachable, and make me worthy of the heavenly kingdom.

Ekos: Vouchsafe my soul, humiliated by many temptations, the ineffable glory, O holy intercessor and singer with the choirs of the fleshless hosts of God. Have mercy and guard me, and illumine my soul with good thoughts, that I may be enriched by thy glory, O my angel; and subdue the enemies that wish me evil, and make me worthy of the heavenly kingdom.

ODE VII

Eirmos: Having gone down to Babylon from Judea, the Children of old by their faith in the Trinity trod down the flame of the furnace while chanting: O God of the fathers, blessed art Thou.

Refrain: Holy Angel of the Lord, my guardian, pray to God for me.

Be merciful to me and entreat God,

O Angel of the Lord; for I have thee as a defender for the whole of my life, a guide and guardian given me by God for ever.

Holy Angel of the Lord, my guardian, pray to God for me.

Leave not my wretched soul, which was given thee blameless by God, to be slain by robbers along the way, O holy Angel, but guide it to the way of repentance.

Glory to the Father, and to the Son, and to the Holy Spirit.

My whole soul is disgraced by the evil thoughts and deeds I have brought upon me, but make haste, O my guide, and grant me healing with good thoughts, that I may be inclined always to the right way.

Both now and ever, and unto the ages of ages. Amen.

O Wisdom of the Most High Personified, for the sake of the Theotokos, fill with wisdom and divine strength all that faithfully cry: O God of our fathers, blessed art Thou.

ODE VIII

Eirmos: The King of heaven, Whom hosts of angels hymn, praise ye and supremely exalt unto all ages.

Refrain: Holy Angel of the Lord, my guardian, pray to God for me.

O good Angel, sent by God, support me, thy servant, in my life and forsake me not unto the ages.

Holy Angel of the Lord, my guardian, pray to God for me.

O most-blessed one, I hymn thee, O good Angel, guide and guardian of my soul unto the ages.

Glory to the Father, and to the Son, and to the Holy Spirit.

Be unto me a protection and fortification in the judgment day of all men, in which all deeds, both good and evil, shall be tried by fire.

Both now and ever, and unto the ages of

ages. Amen.

Be unto me, thy servant, a helper and a calmness, O Ever-Virgin Theotokos, and leave me not bereft of thy protection.

ODE IX

Eirmos: Truly we confess thee to be the Theotokos, we who through thee have been saved, O pure Virgin; with the bodiless choirs, thee do we magnify.

Refrain: O Lord Jesus Christ my God, have mercy on me.

Have mercy on me, O my only Saviour, for Thou art merciful and kindhearted, and make me a member of the choirs of the righteous.

Holy Angel of the Lord, my guardian, pray to God for me.

Grant me ever to think and do what is useful, O Angel of the Lord, that I may be blameless and strong in infirmity.

Glory to the Father, and to the Son, and to the Holy Spirit.

As one having boldness toward the Heavenly King, do thou, with the rest of the bodiless ones, entreat Him to have mercy on me the wretched one.

Both now and ever, and unto the ages of ages. Amen.

Having great boldness toward Him Who took flesh of thee, O Virgin, deliver me from fetters and grant me absolution and salvation through thine intercessions.

Prayer to the Guardian Angel

O holy Angel, my good guardian and protector! With broken heart and ailing soul I stand before thee, entreating: Hearken unto me, thy sinful servant (*Name*); with loud wailing and bitter weeping I cry: Remember not mine iniquity and unrighteousness, through which I a wretched one, have angered thee every day and hour, and have made myself loathsome before our Lord the Creator; show me loving-kindness and leave not me, the defiled, even until mine end. Awaken me from the sleep of sin, and enable me, through thine intercessions, to pass the remaining time of my life without stain, and bring forth fruits worthy of repentance; and above all preserve me from deadly falls into sin, lest I perish in despair, and mine enemy rejoice in my ruin. I know truly and confess with my mouth that there is no other friend and intercessor, protector and champion, such as thou, O holy Angel; for, standing before the throne of the Lord, thou intercedest for me the useless and most sinful of all, lest the Most Good One take my soul in the day of my despair and in a day of evil doing. Cease not, therefore, to entreat mercy of my most kind-hearted Lord and God, that He forgive mine offences, which I have committed throughout all my life, in deed, word, and all my senses, and by judgments which He knoweth, that He save me; that He may chasten me here according to His ineffable mercy, but that He may not expose and put me to trial there in accordance with His simple justice; that He may deem me worthy to bring repentance, and with penitence to worthily receive Divine Communion; for this above all I make entreaty, and I desire such a gift with all my heart. And in the terrible hour of death, be not far from me, my good guardian, driving away the demons of darkness, who have the power to terrify my trembling soul; defend me from their net, when I shall pass through the aerial tollhouses, in order that, being guarded by thee, I may attain the desired paradise, where the choirs of the saints and the celestial hosts unceasingly praise the all-honourable and majestic name in Trinity of God glorified: the Father, the Son, and the Holy Spirit, to Whom is due honour and worship, unto the ages of ages. Amen.

AKATHIST
to our
Sweetest Lord Jesus Christ

Kontakion 1

O Champion Leader and Lord, Vanquisher of hades, I, Thy creature and servant, offer Thee songs of praise, for Thou hast delivered me from eternal death; but as Thou hast unutterable loving-kindness, free me from every danger, as I cry:

Jesus, Son of God, have mercy on me!

Ekos 1

Creator of angels and Lord of hosts, as of old Thou didst open ear and tongue to the deaf and dumb, likewise open now my perplexed mind and tongue to the praise of Thy most holy name, that I may cry to Thee:

Jesus, Most-wonderful, Angels' Astonishment!

Jesus, Most-powerful, Forefathers' Deliverance!

Jesus, Most-sweet, Patriarchs' Exaltation!

Jesus, Most-glorious, Kings' Stronghold!

Jesus, Most-beloved, Prophets' Fulfillment!

Jesus, Most-marvelous, Martyrs' Strength!

Jesus, Most-peaceful, Monks' Joy!

Jesus, Most-gracious, Presbyters' Sweetness!

Jesus, Most-merciful, Fasters' Abstinence!

Jesus, Most-tender, Saints' Rejoicing!

Jesus, Most-honourable, Virgins' Chastity!

Jesus, Everlasting, Sinners' Salvation!

Jesus, Son of God, have mercy on me!

Kontakion 2

As when seeing the widow weeping bitterly, O Lord, Thou wast moved with pity, and didst raise her son from the dead as he was being carried to burial, likewise have pity on me, O Lover of mankind, and raise my soul, deadened by sins, as I cry: Alleluia!

Ekos 2

Seeking to understand the incomprehensible, Philip asked: Lord, show us the Father, and Thou didst answer him: Have I been so long with you and yet hast thou not known that I

am in the Father and the Father in Me?
Likewise, O Incomprehensible One,
with fear I cry to Thee:

Jesus, Eternal God!
Jesus, All-powerful King!
Jesus, Long-suffering Master!
Jesus, All-merciful Saviour!
Jesus, my Gracious Guardian!
Jesus, cleanse my sins!
Jesus, take away mine iniquities!
Jesus, pardon mine unrighteousness!
Jesus, my Hope, forsake me not!
Jesus, my Helper, reject me not!
Jesus, my Creator, forget me not!
Jesus, my Shepherd, destroy me not!
Jesus, Son of God, have mercy on me!

Kontakion 3

Thou Who didst clothe with power
from on high Thine apostles who
tarried in Jerusalem, O Jesus, clothe
also me, stripped bare of all good
works, with the warmth of Thy Holy

Spirit, and grant that with love I may sing to Thee: Alleluia!

Ekos 3

In the abundance of Thy mercy, O Jesus, Thou hast called publicans and sinners and infidels. Now disdain me not who am like them, but as precious myrrh accept this song:

Jesus, Invincible Power!

Jesus, Infinite Mercy!

Jesus, Radiant Beauty!

Jesus, Unspeakable Love!

Jesus, Son of the Living God!

Jesus, have mercy on me a sinner!

Jesus, hear me who was conceived in sins!

Jesus, cleanse me who was born in sins!

Jesus, teach me who am worthless!

Jesus, enlighten my darkness!

Jesus, purify me who am unclean!

Jesus, restore me, a prodigal!

Jesus, Son of God, have mercy on me!

Kontakion 4

Having an interior storm of doubting thoughts, Peter was sinking. But beholding Thee in the flesh walking on the waters, O Jesus, he confessed Thee to be the true God; and receiving the hand of salvation, he cried: Alleluia!

Ekos 4

When the blind man heard Thee, O Lord, passing by on the way, he cried: Jesus, Son of David, have mercy on me! And Thou didst call him and open his eyes. Likewise enlighten the spiritual eyes of my heart with Thy love as I cry to Thee and say:

Jesus, Creator of those on high!

Jesus, Redeemer of those below!

Jesus, Vanquisher of the power of hades!

Jesus, Adorner of every creature!

Jesus, Comforter of my soul!

Jesus, Enlightener of my mind!

Jesus, Gladness of my heart!

Jesus, Health of my body!

Jesus, my Saviour, save me!

Jesus, my Light, enlighten me!

Jesus, deliver me from all torments!

Jesus, save me despite mine unworthiness!

Jesus, Son of God, have mercy on me!

Kontakion 5

As of old Thou didst redeem us from the curse of the law by Thy Divine-flowing Blood, O Jesus, likewise rescue us from the snares in which the serpent hath entangled us through the passions of the flesh, through lustful suggestions, and evil despondency, as we cry unto Thee: Alleluia!

Ekos 5

Having beheld the Creator in human form and knowing Him

to be the Master, the Hebrew children
hastened to please Him with branches,
crying: Hosanna! But we offer Thee a
song, saying:

Jesus, True God!

Jesus, Son of David!

Jesus, Most-glorious King!

Jesus, Blameless Lamb!

Jesus, Most-wonderful Shepherd!

Jesus, Guardian of mine infancy!

Jesus, Nourisher of my youth!

Jesus, Praise of mine old age!

Jesus, my Hope at death!

Jesus, my Life after death!

Jesus, my Comfort at Thy judgment!

Jesus, my Desire, put me not then to
    shame!

Jesus, Son of God, have mercy on me!

Kontakion 6

In fulfillment of the words and mes-
sage of the God-bearing prophets,
O Jesus, Thou didst appear on earth,

and Thou Who art uncontainable
didst dwell with men, and didst take on
our infirmities; being healed through
Thy wounds, we have learned to sing:
Alleluia!

Ekos 6

The light of Thy truth shone upon
the world, and demonic delusion
was driven away; for the idols have fall-
en, O our Saviour, unable to endure
Thy strength. But we, having received
salvation, cry to Thee:

Jesus, the Truth, dispelling falsehood!

Jesus, the Light, above all radiance!

Jesus, the King, surpassing all in
strength!

Jesus, God, constant in mercy!

Jesus, Bread of Life, fill me who am
hungry!

Jesus, Source of Knowledge, give
me to drink who am thirsty!

Jesus, Garment of Gladness, cloth me, the corruptible!

Jesus, Shelter of Joy, cover me, the unworthy!

Jesus, Giver to those that ask, give me sorrow for my sins!

Jesus, Finder of those that seek, find my soul!

Jesus, Opener to those that knock, open my wretched heart!

Jesus, Redeemer of sinners, blot out my transgressions!

Jesus, Son of God, have mercy on me!

Kontakion 7

Desiring to reveal the mystery hidden from the ages, Thou wast led as a sheep to the slaughter, O Jesus, and as a lamb before its shearer. But as God Thou didst rise from the dead and didst ascend with glory to heaven, and along with Thyself Thou didst raise us who cry: Alleluia!

Ekos 7

The Creator hath shown us a marvelous Creature, Who was incarnate of a Virgin without seed, rose from the tomb without breaking the seal, and entered bodily the apostles' room when the doors were shut. Wherefore, marvelling at this, we sing:

Jesus, Infinite Word!

Jesus, Inscrutable Word!

Jesus, Incomprehensible Power!

Jesus, Inconceivable Wisdom!

Jesus, Inexpressible Divinity!

Jesus, Boundless Dominion!

Jesus, Invincible Kingdom!

Jesus, Endless Sovereignty!

Jesus, Supreme Strength!

Jesus, Power Eternal!

Jesus, my Creator, have compassion on me!

Jesus, my Saviour, save me!

Jesus, Son of God, have mercy on me!

Kontakion 8

Seeing God wondrously incarnate, let us shun the vain world and set our mind on things divine; for God came down to earth that He might raise to heaven us who cry to Him: Alleluia!

Ekos 8

The Immeasurable One was below all things, yet in no way separated from things above, when He willingly suffered for our sake, and by His death our death didst put to death, and by His Resurrection didst grant life to those that sing:

Jesus, Sweetness of the heart!

Jesus, Strength of the body!

Jesus, Radiance of the soul!

Jesus, Swiftness of the mind!

Jesus, Joy of the conscience!

Jesus, Well-known Hope!

Jesus, Memory before the ages!

Jesus, High Praise!
Jesus, my Supremely-exalted Glory!
Jesus, my Desire, reject me not!
Jesus, my Shepherd, seek me!
Jesus, my Saviour, save me!
Jesus, Son of God, have mercy on me!

Kontakion 9

All the angelic nature of heaven doth glorify unceasingly Thy most holy name, O Jesus, crying: Holy, Holy, Holy! But we sinners on earth with lips of dust cry: Alleluia!

Ekos 9

We see most eloquent orators voiceless as fish concerning Thee, O Jesus our Saviour; for they are at a loss to say how Thou art perfect man, yet remainest God immutable; but we, marvelling at this mystery, cry faithfully:

Jesus, God before the ages!
Jesus, King of kings!

Jesus, Master of rulers!

Jesus, Judge of the living and the dead!

Jesus, Hope of the hopeless!

Jesus, Comfort of them that mourn!

Jesus, Glory of the poor!

Jesus, condemn me not according to my deeds!

Jesus, cleanse me according to Thy mercy!

Jesus, drive from me despondency!

Jesus, enlighten the thoughts of my heart!

Jesus, grant me remembrance of death!

Jesus, Son of God, have mercy on me!

Kontakion 10

Desiring to save the world, O Sunrise of the East, Thou didst come to the dark Occident of our nature, and didst humble Thyself even unto death; wherefore, Thy name is supremely exalted above every name, and from all the tribes of heaven and earth Thou dost hear: Alleluia!

Ekos 10

King Eternal, Comforter, true Christ! Cleanse us of every stain, as Thou didst cleanse the Ten Lepers; and heal us, as Thou didst heal the greedy soul of Zacchaeus the Publican, that we may shout to Thee in compunction, crying aloud:

Jesus, Treasury Incorruptible!

Jesus, Wealth Unfailing!

Jesus, Strong Food!

Jesus, Drink Inexhaustible!

Jesus, Garment of the poor!

Jesus, Protection of widows!

Jesus, Defender of orphans!

Jesus, Help of toilers!

Jesus, Guide of pilgrims!

Jesus, Pilot of voyagers!

Jesus, Calmer of tempests!

Jesus, God, raise me who am fallen!
Jesus, Son of God, have mercy on me!

Kontakion 11

Tenderest songs I, though unworthy, offer to Thee, and like the woman of Canaan, I cry unto Thee: O Jesus, have mercy on me! For it is not a daughter, but my flesh cruelly possessed with passions and burning with fury. So grant healing to me who cry unto Thee: Alleluia.

Ekos 11

Having previously persecuted Thee, the Light-bestowing Lamp of those in the darkness of ignorance, Paul heeded the power of the voice of Divine enlightenment, and understood the swiftness of the soul's conversion; thus also do Thou enlighten the dark eye of my soul, as I cry:
Jesus, my Most-mighty King!

Jesus, my Most-powerful God!

Jesus, mine Immortal Lord!

Jesus, my Most-glorious Creator!

Jesus, my Most-good Guide!

Jesus, my Most-compassionate Shepherd!

Jesus, my Most-merciful Master!

Jesus, my Most-gracious Saviour!

Jesus, enlighten my senses darkened by passions!

Jesus, heal my body scabbed with sins!

Jesus, cleanse my mind of vain thoughts!

Jesus, keep my heart from evil desires!

Jesus, Son of God, have mercy on me!

Kontakion 12

Grant me Thy grace, O Jesus, Absolver of all debts, and receive me who am repenting, as Thou didst receive Peter who denied Thee, and call me who am downcast, as of old Thou didst call Paul who persecuted Thee, and hear me crying to Thee: Alleluia!

Ekos 12

Praising Thine incarnation, we all extol Thee, and we believe with Thomas that Thou art Lord and God, sitting with the Father and coming to judge the living and the dead. Vouchsafe me then to stand on Thy right hand, who now cry:

Jesus, King before the ages, have mercy on me.

Jesus, Sweet-scented Flower, make me fragrant!

Jesus, Beloved Warmth, make me fervent!

Jesus, Eternal Temple, shelter me!

Jesus, Garment of Light, adorn me!

Jesus, Pearl of Great Price, irradiate me!

Jesus, Precious Stone, illumine me!

Jesus, Sun of Righteousness, shine on me!

Jesus, Holy Light, make me radiant!

Jesus, from sickness of soul and body deliver me!

Jesus, from the hands of the adversary rescue me!

Jesus, from the unquenchable fire and other eternal torments save me!

Jesus, Son of God, have mercy on me!

Kontakion 13

O most-sweet and all-compassionate Jesus! Receive now this our small supplication, as Thou didst receive the widow's two mites, and keep Thine inheritance from all enemies, visible and invisible, from foreign invasion, from disease and famine, from all tribulations and mortal wounds, and rescue from the torment

to come all that cry to Thee: Alleluia!
This is said thrice. Then:

Ekos 1

Creator of angels and Lord of hosts, as of old Thou didst open ear and tongue to the deaf and dumb, likewise open now my perplexed mind and tongue to the praise of Thy most holy name, that I may cry to Thee:

Jesus, Most-wonderful, Angels' Astonishment!

Jesus, Most-powerful, Forefathers' Deliverance!

Jesus, Most-sweet, Patriarchs' Exaltation!

Jesus, Most-glorious, Kings' Stronghold!

Jesus, Most-beloved, Prophets' Fulfillment!

Jesus, Most-marvelous, Martyrs' Strength!

Jesus, Most-peaceful, Monks' Joy!

Jesus, Most-gracious, Presbyters' Sweetness!

Jesus, Most-merciful, Fasters' Abstinence!

Jesus, Most-tender, Saints' Rejoicing!

Jesus, Most-honourable, Virgins' Chastity!

Jesus, Everlasting, Sinners' Salvation!

Jesus, Son of God, have mercy on me!

Kontakion 1

O Champion Leader and Lord, Vanquisher of hades, I, Thy creature and servant, offer Thee songs of praise, for Thou hast delivered me from eternal death; but as Thou hast unutterable loving-kindness, free me from every danger, as I cry:

Jesus, Son of God, have mercy on me!

Prayer to Our Lord Jesus Christ

To Thee, O Lord, the only Good One, Who rememberest not evils, I confess my sins, I fall down before Thee, unworthy that I am, crying out: I have sinned, O Lord, I have sinned, and I am not worthy to look upon the height of heaven for the multitude of mine iniquities. But, my Lord, O Lord, grant me tears of compunction, Thou Who alone art good and merciful, so that with them I may entreat Thee to cleanse me of all sin before the end; for frightful and terrible is the place that I must pass through when I have separated from this body, and a multitude of dark and inhuman demons awaiteth me, and there is no one to come to my help or to deliver me; wherefore, I fall down before Thy goodness: deliver me not up to them that wrong me, nor let mine enemies triumph over me, O Good Lord, nor let them say: thou hast come into our hands, and thou hast been delivered unto us. Neither, O Lord, forget Thy compassions, and render not unto me according to mine iniquities, and turn not Thy countenance away from me; but do Thou, O Lord, chasten me, but with mercy and compassion, and let not mine enemy rejoice over me, but quench his threatening against me, and bring to nought all his deeds. And grant me an unsullied way to Thee, O Good Lord, because, having sinned, I have not had recourse to any other physician, and have not stretched out my hands to a strange god. Therefore, reject not my supplication, but heark-en unto me in Thy goodness, and strengthen my heart in Thy fear; and let Thy grace be upon me, O Lord, like a fire consuming the impure thoughts within me. For Thou, O Lord, art the Light above all lights, the Joy above all joys, the Repose above all repose, the True Life, and the Salvation that abideth unto the ages of ages. Amen.

AKATHIST
to Our Most Holy Lady the Theotokos

Kontakion 1

To Thee, the Champion Leader, we thy servants dedicate a feast of victory and of thanksgiving as ones rescued out of sufferings, O Theotokos; but as thou art one with might which is invincible, from all dangers that can be do thou deliver us, that we may cry to thee:

Rejoice, thou Bride Unwedded!

Ekos 1

An archangel was sent from heaven to say to the Theotokos: Rejoice! And beholding Thee, O Lord, taking bodily form, he was amazed and with his bodiless voice he stood crying to her such things as these:

Rejoice, thou through whom joy will shine forth!

Rejoice, thou through whom the curse will cease!

Rejoice, recall of fallen Adam!

Rejoice, redemption of the tears of Eve!

Rejoice, height inaccessible to human thought!

Rejoice, depth indiscernible even for the eyes of angels!

Rejoice, for thou art the King's throne!

Rejoice, for thou bearest Him Who beareth all!

Rejoice, star that causest the Sun to
    appear!

Rejoice, womb of the Divine Incar-
    nation!

Rejoice, thou through whom cre-
    ation is renewed!

Rejoice, thou through whom we
    worship the Creator!

Rejoice, thou Bride Unwedded!

Kontakion 2

Seeing herself to be chaste, the holy
one said boldly to Gabriel: The
marvel of thy speech is difficult for my
soul to accept. How canst thou speak
of a birth from a seedless conception?
And she cried: Alleluia.

Ekos 2

Seeking to know knowledge that
cannot be known, the Virgin cried
to the ministering one: Tell me, how
can a son be born from a chaste womb?
Then he spake to her in fear, only cry-

ing aloud thus:

Rejoice, initiate of God's ineffable will!

Rejoice, assurance of those who pray in silence!

Rejoice, beginning of Christ's miracles!

Rejoice, crown of His dogmas!

Rejoice, heavenly ladder by which God came down!

Rejoice, bridge that conveyest us from earth to heaven!

Rejoice, wonder of angels sounded abroad!

Rejoice, wound of demons bewailed afar!

Rejoice, thou who ineffably gavest birth to the Light!

Rejoice, thou who didst reveal thy secret to none!

Rejoice, thou who surpassest the knowledge of the wise!

Rejoice, thou who givest light to the minds of the faithful!
Rejoice, thou Bride Unwedded!

Kontakion 3

The power of the Most High then overshadowed the Virgin for conception, and showed her fruitful womb as a sweet meadow to all who wish to reap salvation, as they sing: Alleluia!

Ekos 3

Having received God into her womb, the Virgin hastened to Elizabeth whose unborn babe at once recognized her embrace, rejoiced, and with leaps of joy as songs, cried to the Theotokos:

Rejoice, branch of an Unfading Sprout!
Rejoice, acquisition of Immortal Fruit!
Rejoice, labourer that labourest for the Lover of mankind!

Rejoice, thou who gavest birth to the Planter of our life!

Rejoice, cornland yielding a rich crop of mercies!

Rejoice, table bearing a wealth of forgiveness!

Rejoice, thou who makest to bloom the garden of delight!

Rejoice, thou who preparest a haven for souls!

Rejoice, acceptable incense of intercession!

Rejoice, propitiation of all the world!

Rejoice, good will of God to mortals!

Rejoice, boldness of mortals before God!

Rejoice, thou Bride Unwedded!

Kontakion 4

Having within a tempest of doubting thoughts, the chaste Joseph was troubled. For knowing thee to have no husband, he suspected a secret union, O blameless one. But having learned that thy conception was of the Holy Spirit, he said: Alleluia!

Ekos 4

While the angels were chanting, the shepherds heard of Christ's coming in the flesh, and having run to the Shepherd, they beheld Him as a blameless Lamb that had been pastured in Mary's womb, and singing to her they cried:

Rejoice, Mother of the Lamb and the Shepherd!

Rejoice, fold of rational sheep!

Rejoice, torment of invisible enemies!

Rejoice, opening of the gates of paradise!

Rejoice, for the things of heaven rejoice with the earth!

Rejoice, for the things of earth join

chorus with the heavens!

Rejoice, never-silent mouth of the apostles!

Rejoice, invincible courage of the passion-bearers!

Rejoice, firm support of faith!

Rejoice, radiant token of grace!

Rejoice, thou through whom hades was stripped bare!

Rejoice, thou through whom we are clothed with glory!

Rejoice, thou Bride Unwedded!

Kontakion 5

Having sighted the divinely-moving star, the Magi followed its radiance; and holding it as a lamp, by it they sought a powerful King; and having reached the Unreachable One, they rejoiced, shouting to Him: Alleluia!

Ekos 5

The sons of the Chaldees saw in the hands of the Virgin Him Who with

His hand made man. And knowing Him to be the Master, even though He had taken the form of a servant, they hastened to serve Him with gifts, and to cry to her who is blessed:

Rejoice, Mother of the Unsetting Star!

Rejoice, dawn of the mystic day!

Rejoice, thou who didst extinguish the furnace of error!

Rejoice, thou who didst enlighten the initiates of the Trinity!

Rejoice, thou who didst banish from power the inhuman tyrant!

Rejoice, thou who didst show us Christ the Lord, the Lover of mankind!

Rejoice, thou who redeemest from pagan worship!

Rejoice, thou who dost drag us from the works of mire!

Rejoice, thou who didst quench the worship of fire!

Rejoice, thou who rescuest from the flame of the passions!

Rejoice, guide of the faithful to chastity!

Rejoice, gladness of all generations!

Rejoice, thou Bride Unwedded!

Kontakion 6

Having become God-bearing heralds, the Magi returned to Babylon, having fulfilled Thy prophecy; and having preached Thee to all as the Christ, they left Herod as a babbler who knew not how to sing: Alleluia!

Ekos 6

By shining in Egypt the light of truth, Thou didst dispel the darkness of falsehood; for its idols fell, O Saviour, unable to endure Thy strength; and those who were delivered from them cried to the Theotokos:

Rejoice, uplifting of men!
Rejoice, downfall of demons!
Rejoice, thou who didst trample
down the dominion of
delusion!
Rejoice, thou who didst unmask the
fraud of idols!
Rejoice, sea that didst drown the
Pharaoh of the mind!
Rejoice, rock that dost refresh those
thirsting for life!
Rejoice, pillar of fire that guidest
those in darkness!
Rejoice, shelter of the world broad-
er than a cloud!
Rejoice, sustenance replacing manna!
Rejoice, minister of holy delight!
Rejoice, land of promise!
Rejoice, thou from whom floweth
milk and honey!
Rejoice, thou Bride Unwedded!

Kontakion 7

When Symeon was about to depart this age of delusion, Thou wast brought as a Babe to him, but Thou wast recognized by him as perfect God also; wherefore, marvelling at Thine ineffable wisdom, he cried: Alleluia!

Ekos 7

The Creator showed us a new creation when He appeared to us who come from Him. For He sprang from a seedless womb, and kept it incorrupt as it was, that seeing the mir-acle we might sing to her, crying out:

Rejoice, flower of incorruptibility!

Rejoice, crown of continence!

Rejoice, thou from whom shineth the Archetype of the resurrection!

Rejoice, thou who revealest the life of the angels!

Rejoice, tree of shining fruit whereby the faithful are nourished!

Rejoice, tree of goodly shade by which many are sheltered!

Rejoice, thou that hast carried in thy womb the Redeemer of captives!

Rejoice, thou that gavest birth to the Guide of those astray!

Rejoice, supplication before the Righteous Judge!

Rejoice, forgiveness of many sins!

Rejoice, robe of boldness for the naked!

Rejoice, love that vanquishest all desire!

Rejoice, thou Bride Unwedded!

Kontakion 8

Having beheld a strange nativity, let us estrange ourselves from the world and transport our minds to heaven; for the Most High God appeared on earth as a lowly man, because He wished to draw to the heights them that cry to Him: Alleluia!

Ekos 8

Wholly present was the Inexpressible Word among those here below, yet in no way absent from those on high; for this was a divine condescension and not a change of place, and His birth was from a God-receiving Virgin who heard these things:

Rejoice, container of the Uncontainable God!

Rejoice, door of solemn mystery!

Rejoice, report doubtful to unbelievers!

Rejoice, undoubted boast of the faithful!

Rejoice, all-holy chariot of Him Who sitteth upon the Cherubim!

Rejoice, all-glorious temple of Him Who is above the Seraphim!

Rejoice, thou who hast united opposites!

Rejoice, thou who hast joined virginity and motherhood!

Rejoice, thou through whom transgression hath been absolved!

Rejoice, thou through whom paradise is opened!

Rejoice, key to the kingdom of Christ!

Rejoice, hope of eternal good things!

Rejoice, thou Bride Unwedded!

Kontakion 9

All the angels were amazed at the great act of Thine incarnation; for they saw the Unapproachable God as a man approachable to all, abiding with us, and hearing from all: Alleluia!

Ekos 9

We see most eloquent orators mute as fish before thee, O Theotokos, for they are at a loss to tell how thou remainest a Virgin and couldst bear a child. But we, marvelling at this mystery, cry out faithfully:

Rejoice, receptacle of the Wisdom of God!

Rejoice, treasury of His Providence!

Rejoice, thou who showest philosophers to be fools!

Rejoice, thou who exposest the learned as irrational!

Rejoice, for the clever critics have become foolish!

Rejoice, for the writers of myths have faded away!

Rejoice, thou who didst rend the webs of the Athenians!

Rejoice, thou who didst fill the nets of the fishermen!

Rejoice, thou who drawest us from the depths of ignorance!

Rejoice, thou who enlightenest many with knowledge!

Rejoice, ship for those who wish to
be saved!

Rejoice, harbor for sailors on the
sea of life!

Rejoice, thou Bride Unwedded!

Kontakion 10

Desiring to save the world, He that
is the Creator of all came to it
according to His Own promise, and
He that, as God, is the Shepherd, for
our sake appeared unto us as a man;
for, like calling unto like, as God He
heareth: Alleluia!

Ekos 10

A bulwark art thou to virgins, and
to all that flee unto thee, O
Virgin Theotokos; for the Maker of
heaven and earth prepared thee, O
most pure one, dwelt in thy womb, and
taught all to call to thee:

Rejoice, pillar of virginity!

Rejoice, gate of salvation!

Rejoice, leader of mental formation!

Rejoice, bestower of divine good!

Rejoice, for thou didst renew those conceived in shame!

Rejoice, for thou gavest understanding to those robbed of their minds!

Rejoice, thou who didst foil the corrupter of minds!

Rejoice, thou who gavest birth to the Sower of purity!

Rejoice, bridechamber of a seedless marriage!

Rejoice, thou who dost wed the faithful to the Lord!

Rejoice, good nourisher of virgins!

Rejoice, adorner of holy souls as for marriage!

Rejoice, thou Bride Unwedded!

Kontakion 11

Every hymn is defeated that trieth to encompass the multitude of Thy many compassions; for if we offer to Thee, O Holy King, songs equal in number to the sand, nothing have we done worthy of that which Thou hast given us who shout to Thee: Alleluia!

Ekos 11

We behold the holy Virgin, a shining lamp appearing to those in darkness; for, kindling the Immaterial Light, she guideth all to divine knowledge, she illumineth minds with radiance, and is honoured by our shouting these things:

Rejoice, ray of the noetic Sun!

Rejoice, radiance of the Unsetting Light!

Rejoice, lightning that enlightenest our souls!

Rejoice, thunder that terrifiest our enemies!

Rejoice, for thou didst cause the Refulgent Light to dawn!

Rejoice, for thou didst cause the river of many streams to gush forth!

Rejoice, thou who paintest the image of the font!

Rejoice, thou who blottest out the stain of sin!

Rejoice, laver that washest the conscience clean!

Rejoice, cup that drawest up joy!

Rejoice, aroma of the sweet fragrance of Christ!

Rejoice, life of mystical gladness!

Rejoice, thou Bride Unwedded!

Kontakion 12

When the Absolver of all mankind desired to blot out ancient debts, of His Own will He came to dwell among those who had fallen from His grace; and having torn up the handwriting of their sins, He heareth this from all: Alleluia!

Ekos 12

While singing to thine Offspring, we all praise thee as a living temple, O Theotokos; for the Lord Who holdeth all things in His hand dwelt in thy womb, and He sanctified and glorified thee, and taught all to cry to thee:

Rejoice, tabernacle of God the Word!

Rejoice, saint greater than the saints!

Rejoice, ark gilded by the Spirit!

Rejoice, inexhaustible treasury of life!

Rejoice, precious diadem of pious kings!

Rejoice, venerable boast of reverent priests!

Rejoice, unshakable fortress of the Church!

Rejoice, inviolable wall of the kingdom!

Rejoice, thou through whom victo-
ries are obtained!

Rejoice, thou through whom foes
fall prostrate!

Rejoice, healing of my flesh!

Rejoice, salvation of my soul!

Rejoice, thou Bride Unwedded!

Kontakion 13

O all-praised Mother who didst bear the Word holiest of all the saints, accept now our offering, and deliver us from all misfortune, and rescue from the torment to come those that cry to thee: Alleluia! *This kontakion we say thrice. Then:*

Ekos 1

An archangel was sent from heaven to say to the Theotokos: Rejoice! And beholding Thee, O Lord, taking bodily form, he was amazed and with his bodiless voice he stood crying to her such things as these:

Rejoice, thou through whom joy will shine forth!

Rejoice, thou through whom the curse will cease!

Rejoice, recall of fallen Adam!

Rejoice, redemption of the tears of Eve!

Rejoice, height inaccessible to human thought!

Rejoice, depth indiscernible even for the eyes of angels!

Rejoice, for thou art the King's throne!

Rejoice, for thou bearest Him Who beareth all!

Rejoice, star that causest the Sun to appear!

Rejoice, womb of the Divine Incarnation!

Rejoice, thou through whom creation is renewed!

Rejoice, thou through whom we

worship the Creator!
Rejoice, thou Bride Unwedded!

Kontakion 1

To Thee, the Champion Leader, we thy servants dedicate a feast of victory and of thanksgiving as ones rescued out of sufferings, O Theotokos; but as thou art one with might which is invincible, from all dangers that can be do thou deliver us, that we may cry to thee:

Rejoice, thou Bride Unwedded!

Prayer to the Most Holy Theotokos

O most holy Sovereign Lady Theotokos! Higher art thou than all the angels and archangels, and more honourable than all creation, a helper of the wronged art thou, the hope of the hopeless, an intercessor for the poor, the consolation of the sorrowful, a nourisher of the hungry, a robe for the naked, healing for the sick, the salvation of sinners, the help and protection of all Christians. O all-merciful Sovereign Lady Virgin Theotokos! Through thy mercy save and have mercy on the most holy Orthodox patriarchs, the most holy metropolitans, archbishops and bishops, and all the priestly and monastic orders, the military leaders, civic leaders, and Christ-loving armed forces, and well-wishers, and all Orthodox Christians do thou defend by thy precious omophorion, and entreat, O Lady, Christ our God Who was incarnate of thee without seed, that He gird us with His power from on high against our enemies, visible and invisible, O all-merciful Sovereign Lady Theotokos! Raise us up out of the depths of sin, and deliver us from famine, destruction, from earthquake and flood, from fire and the sword, from invasion of aliens and civil war, and from sudden death, and from noxious winds, and from death-bearing plagues, and from all evil. Grant, O Lady, peace and health to thy servants, all Orthodox Christians, and enlighten their minds, and the eyes of their hearts unto salvation; and vouchsafe unto us, thy sinful servants, the kingdom of thy Son, Christ our God: for blessed and most-glorified is His dominion, together with His unoriginate Father, and His Most-holy and good and life-creating Spirit, now and ever, and unto the ages of ages. Amen.

CANON OF REPENTANCE
To our Lord Jesus Christ
Sixth Tone. ODE I

Eirmos: When Israel walked on foot in the deep as on dry land, on seeing their pursuer Pharaoh drowned, they cried: Let us sing to God a song of victory.

Have mercy on me, O God, have mercy on me.

Now I, a burdened sinner, have approached Thee, my Lord and God. But I dare not raise mine eyes to heaven. I only pray, saying: Give me, O Lord, understanding, that I may weep bitterly over my deeds.

Have mercy on me, O God, have mercy on me.

O woe is me, a sinner! Wretched am I above all men. There is no repentance in me. Give me, O Lord, tears, that I may weep bitterly over my deeds.

Glory to the Father, and to the Son, and to the Holy Spirit.

Foolish, wretched man, thou art wasting thy time in idleness! Think of thy life and turn to the Lord God, and weep bitterly over thy deeds.

Both now and ever, and unto the ages of ages. Amen.

Theotokion: O most pure Mother of God, look upon me a sinner, and deliver me from the snares of the devil, and guide me to the way of repentance, that I may weep bitterly over my deeds.

ODE III

Eirmos: There is none holy as Thou, O Lord my God, Who hast exalted the horn of Thy faithful, O Good One, and hast established us upon the rock of Thy confession.

Have mercy on me, O God, have mercy on me.

When the thrones will be set at the dread judgment, then the deeds of all men shall be laid bare. There will be woe for sinners being sent to torment! And knowing that, my soul, repent of thine evil deeds.

Have mercy on me, O God, have mercy on me.

The righteous shall rejoice, but the sinners will weep. Then no one will be able to help us, but our deeds will condemn us. Wherefore, before the end, repent of thine evil deeds.

Glory to the Father, and to the Son, and to the Holy Spirit.

Alas for me, a great sinner, who have defiled myself by my deeds and thoughts. Not a teardrop do I have, because of my hardheartedness. But now, rise from the earth, my soul, and repent of thine evil deeds.

Both now and ever, and unto the ages of ages. Amen.

Theotokion: Behold, thy Son calleth, O Lady, and directeth us to what is good, yet I a sinner always flee from the good. But do thou, O merciful one, have mercy on me, that I may repent of mine evil deeds.

Lord, have mercy. *Thrice.*

Sessional Hymn, Sixth Tone:

I think of the terrible day and weep over mine evil deeds. How shall I answer the Immortal King? With what boldness shall I, a prodigal, look at the Judge? O compassionate Father, O Only-begotten Son, and Holy Spirit, have mercy on me.

Glory to the Father, and to the Son, and to the Holy Spirit, both now and ever, and unto the ages of ages. Amen.

Theotokion: Bound now with many fetters of sins, and held fast by cruel passions, I flee unto thee, my salvation, and cry aloud: Help me, O Virgin Mother of God.

ODE IV

Eirmos: Christ is my power, my God and my Lord, doth the august Church sing in godly fashion, and she doth cry out with a pure mind, keeping festival in the Lord.

Have mercy on me, O God, have mercy on me.

Broad is the way here and convenient for indulging in pleasures, but how bitter it will be on the last day when the soul is separated from the body! Beware of these things, O man, for the sake of the kingdom of God.

Have mercy on me, O God, have mercy on me.

Why dost thou wrong the poor man? Why dost thou withhold the wage of the hired servant? Why dost thou not love thy brother? Why dost thou pursue lust and pride? Therefore, abandon these things, my soul, and repent for the sake of the kingdom of God.

Glory to the Father, and to the Son, and to the Holy Spirit.

O mindless man! How long wilt

thou busy thyself like a bee, collecting thy wealth? For it will soon perish like dust and ashes. But seek rather the kingdom of God.

Both now and ever, and unto the ages of ages. Amen.

Theotokion: O Lady Theotokos, have mercy on me, a sinner, and strengthen and keep me in virtue, lest sudden death snatch me away unprepared; and lead me, O Virgin, to the kingdom of God.

ODE V

Eirmos: With Thy divine light, O Good One, illumine the souls of them that rise early to pray to Thee with love, I pray, that they may know Thee, O Word of God, as the true God, Who recalleth us from the darkness of sin.

Have mercy on me, O God, have mercy on me.

Remember, wretched man, how thou art enslaved to lies, slander, theft, infirmities, wild beasts, on account of sins. O my sinful soul, is this what thou hast desired?

Have mercy on me, O God, have mercy on me.

My members tremble, for with all of them I have done wrong: with mine eyes in looking, with mine ears in hearing, with my tongue in speaking evil, and by surrendering the whole of myself to Gehenna. O my sinful soul, is this what thou hast desired?

Glory to the Father, and to the Son, and to the Holy Spirit.

Thou didst receive the prodigal and the thief who repented, O Saviour, and I alone have succumbed to sinful sloth and have become enslaved to evil deeds. O my sinful soul, is this what thou hast desired?

Both now and ever, and unto the ages of ages. Amen.

Theotokion: Wonderful and speedy helper of all men, help me, O Mother of God, unworthy as I am, for my sinful soul hath desired this.

ODE VI

Eirmos: Beholding the sea of life surging with the tempest of temptations, I run to Thy calm haven and cry unto Thee: Raise up my life from corruption, O Greatly-merciful One.

Have mercy on me, O God, have mercy on me.

I have lived my life wantonly on earth and have given my soul over to darkness. But now I implore Thee, O merciful Master, free me from this work of the enemy and give me the knowledge to do Thy will.

Have mercy on me, O God, have mercy on me.

Who doeth such things as I do? For like a swine lying in the mud, so do I serve sin. But do Thou, O Lord, pull me out of this vileness and give me the heart to do Thy commandments.

Glory to the Father, and to the Son, and to the Holy Spirit.

Rise, wretched man, to God and, remembering thy sins, fall down before the Creator, weeping and groaning, for He is merciful and will grant thee to know His will.

Both now and ever, and unto the ages of ages. Amen.

Theotokion: O Virgin Theotokos, protect me from evil visible and invisible, O immaculate one, and accept my prayers and present them to thy Son, that He may grant me the mind to do His will.

Lord, have mercy. *Thrice.*

Glory to the Father, and to the Son, and to the Holy Spirit, both now and ever, and unto the ages of ages. Amen.

Kontakion: O my soul, why dost thou become rich in sins? Why dost thou do the will of the devil? On what dost thou set thy hope? Cease from these things and turn to God with weeping, and cry out: O kindhearted Lord, have mercy on me a sinner.

Ekos: Think, my soul, of the bitter hour of death and the judgment day of thy God and Creator.   For terrible angels will seize thee, my soul, and will lead thee into the eternal fire. And so, before thy death, repent and cry: O Lord, have mercy on me a sinner.

ODE VII

Eirmos: An angel made the furnace sprinkle dew on the righteous youths. But the command of God consumed the Chaldeans and prevailed upon the tyrant to cry: Blessed art Thou, O God of our fathers.

Have mercy on me, O God, have mercy on me.

Put not thy hope, my soul, in corruptible wealth, and in what is unjustly collected. For thou dost not know to whom thou wilt leave it all. But cry aloud: Have mercy, O Christ God, on me the unworthy.

Have mercy on me, O God, have mercy on me.

Trust not, my soul, in health of body and quickly-passing beauty. For thou seest that the strong and the young die. But cry aloud: Have mercy, O Christ God, on me the unworthy.

Glory to the Father, and to the Son, and to the Holy Spirit.

Remember, my soul, eternal life and the heavenly kingdom prepared for the saints, and the outer darkness and the wrath of God for the evil, and cry: Have mercy, O Christ God, on me the unworthy.

Both now and ever, and unto the ages of ages. Amen.

Theotokion: Fall down, my soul, before the Mother of God, and pray to her; for she is the quick helper of those that repent. She entreateth the Son, Christ God, and hath mercy on me the unworthy.

ODE VIII

Eirmos: From the flame Thou didst sprinkle dew upon the Saints, and didst burn the sacrifice of a righteous man which was sprinkled with water. For Thou alone, O Christ, dost do all as Thou willest. Thee do we exalt unto all ages.

Have mercy on me, O God, have mercy on me.

How shall I not weep when I think of death? For I have seen my brother in his coffin, without glory or comeliness. What, then, do I expect? And what do I hope for? Only grant me, O Lord, repentance before the end.

Have mercy on me, O God, have mercy on me.

How shall I not weep.... *(Repeat).*

Glory to the Father, and to the Son, and to the Holy Spirit.

I believe that Thou wilt come to judge the living and the dead, and that all will stand in order, old and young, lords and princes, priests and virgins. Where shall I find myself? Therefore, I cry: Grant me, O Lord, repentance before the end.

Both now and ever, and unto the ages of ages. Amen.

Theotokion: O most pure Theotokos, accept mine unworthy prayer and preserve me from sudden death, and grant me repentance before the end.

ODE IX

Eirmos: It is not possible for men to see God, on Whom the ranks of angels dare not gaze; but through thee, O all-pure one, appeared to men the Word incarnate, Whom magnifying, with the heavenly hosts we call thee blessed.

Have mercy on me, O God, have mercy on me.

Now I flee unto you, ye Angels, Archangels, and all the heavenly hosts who stand at the throne of God: pray to your Creator that He may deliver my soul from eternal torment.

Have mercy on me, O God, have mercy on me.

Now I turn to you with tears, holy patriarchs, kings and prophets, apostles and holy hierarchs, and all the elect of Christ: help me at the judgment, that He may save my soul from the power of the enemy.

Glory to the Father, and to the Son, and to the Holy Spirit.

Now I lift up my hands to you, holy martyrs, hermits, virgins, righteous ones and all the saints, who pray to the Lord for the whole world, that He may have mercy on me at the hour of my death.

Both now and ever, and unto the ages of ages. Amen.

Theotokion: O Mother of God, help me who have strong hope in thee; implore thy Son that He may place me the unworthy on His right hand, when He sitteth to judge the living and the dead. Amen.

PRAYER AFTER THE CANON

O Master Christ God, Who hast healed my passions through Thy Passion, and hast cured my wounds through Thy wounds: Grant me, who have sinned greatly against Thee, tears of compunction. Transform my body with the fragrance of Thy life-giving Body, and sweeten my soul with Thy precious Blood from the bitterness with which the foe hath fed me. Lift up my downcast mind to Thee, and take it out of the abyss of perdition, for I have no repentance, I have no compunction, I have no consoling tears which uplift children to their heritage. My mind hath been darkened through earthly passions, I cannot look up to Thee in pain, I cannot warm myself with tears of love for Thee. But, O Sovereign Lord Jesus Christ, Treasury of good things, give me thorough repentance and a diligent heart to seek Thee; grant me Thy grace, and renew in me the likeness of Thine image. I have forsaken Thee—do Thou not forsake me! Come out to seek me; lead me up to Thy pasturage and number me among the sheep of Thy chosen flock. Nourish me with them on the grass of Thy Holy Mysteries, through the intercessions of Thy most pure Mother and all Thy saints. Amen.

THE ORDER OF PREPARATION
FOR HOLY COMMUNION

Through the prayers of our holy fathers, O Lord Jesus Christ our God, have mercy on us. Amen.

Glory to Thee, our God, glory to Thee.

O Heavenly King.... *Trisagion*.... Glory.... Both now.... O Most Holy Trinity.... Lord, have mercy, *thrice*. Glory.... Both now.... Our Father.... Lord, have mercy, *twelve.* Glory.... Both now.... O come let us worship..., *thrice. And these Psalms:*

PSALM 22

The Lord is my shepherd, and I shall not want. In a place of green pasture, there hath He made me to dwell; beside the water of rest hath He nurtured me. He hath converted my soul, He hath led me on the paths of righteousness for His name's sake. For though I should walk in the midst of the shadow of death, I will fear no evil, for Thou art with me; Thy rod and Thy staff, they have comforted me. Thou hast prepared a table before me in the presence of them that afflict me. Thou hast anointed my head with oil, and Thy cup which filleth me, how excellent it is! And Thy mercy shall pursue me all the days of my life, and I will dwell in the house of the Lord unto length of days.

PSALM 23

The earth is the Lord's, and the fulness thereof, the world, and all that dwell therein. He hath founded it upon the seas, and upon the rivers hath He prepared it. Who shall ascend into the mountain of the Lord? Or who shall stand in His holy place? He that is innocent in hands and pure in heart, who hath not received his soul in vain, and hath not sworn deceitfully to his neighbour. Such a one shall receive a blessing from the Lord, and mercy from God his Saviour. This is the generation of them that seek the Lord, of them that seek the face of the God of Jacob. Lift up your gates, O ye princes; and be ye lifted up, ye ever-lasting gates, and the King of Glory shall enter in. Who is this King of Glory? The Lord strong and mighty, the Lord, mighty in war. Lift up your gates, O ye princes; and be ye lifted up, ye everlasting gates, and the King of Glory shall enter in. Who is this King of Glory? The Lord of hosts, He is the King of Glory.

PSALM 115

I believed, wherefore I spake; I was humbled exceedingly. As for me, I said in mine ecstasy; Every man is a liar. What shall I render unto the Lord for all that He hath rendered unto me? I will take the cup of salvation, and I will call upon the name of the Lord. My vows unto the Lord will I pay in the presence of all His people. Precious in the sight of the Lord is the death of His saints. O Lord, I am Thy servant; I am Thy servant and the son of Thy handmaid. Thou hast broken my bonds asunder. I will sacrifice a sacrifice of praise unto Thee, and I will call upon the name of the Lord. My vows unto the Lord will I pay in the presence of all His people, in the courts of the house of the Lord, in the midst of thee, O Jerusalem.

Glory to the Father, and to the Son,

and to the Holy Spirit, both now and ever, and unto the ages of ages. Amen.

Alleluia, alleluia, alleluia. Glory to Thee, O God. *Thrice.*

Lord, have mercy. *Thrice.*

Troparia, Eighth Tone: Disregard my transgressions, O Lord Who wast born of a Virgin, and purify my heart, and make it a temple for Thy spotless Body and Blood. Let me not be rejected from Thy presence, O Thou Who hast great mercy without meassure.

Glory to the Father, and to the Son, and to the Holy Spirit.

How can I who am unworthy dare to come to the Communion of Thy Holy Things? For if I should dare to approach Thee with those that are worthy, my garment betrayeth me, for it is not a festal robe, and I shall cause the condemnation of my greatly-sinful soul. Cleanse, O Lord, the pollution from my soul, and save me, as Thou art the Lover of mankind.

Both now and ever, and unto the ages of ages. Amen.

Greatly multiplied, O Theotokos, are my sins; unto thee have I fled, O pure one, imploring salvation. Do thou visit mine enfeebled soul, and pray to thy Son and our God that He grant me forgiveness for the evil I have done, O thou only blessed one.

During Holy and Great Lent say this:

When the glorious disciples were enlightened at the washing of the feet, then Judas the ungodly one was stricken and darkened with the love of silver. And unto the lawless judges did he deliver Thee, the Righteous Judge. Behold, O lover of money, him that for the sake thereof did hang himself; flee from that insatiable soul that dared such things against the Master. O Thou Who art good unto all, Lord, glory be to Thee.

PSALM 50

Have mercy on me, O God, according to Thy great mercy; and according to the multitude of Thy compassions blot out my transgression. Wash me thoroughly from mine iniquity, and cleanse me from my sin. For I know mine iniquity, and my sin is ever before me. Against Thee only have I sinned and done this evil before Thee, that Thou mightest be justified in Thy words, and prevail when Thou art judged. For behold, I was conceived in iniquities, and in sins did my mother bear me. For behold, Thou hast loved truth; the hidden and secret things of Thy wisdom hast Thou made manifest unto me. Thou shalt sprinkle me with hyssop, and I shall be made clean; Thou shalt wash me, and I shall be made whiter than snow. Thou shalt make me to hear joy and gladness; the bones that be humbled, they shall rejoice. Turn Thy face away from my sins, and blot out all mine iniquities. Create in me a clean heart, O God, and renew a right spirit within me. Cast me not away from Thy presence, and take not Thy Holy Spirit from me. Restore unto me the joy of Thy salvation, and with Thy governing Spirit establish me. I shall teach transgressors Thy ways, and the ungodly shall turn back unto Thee. Deliver me from blood-guiltiness, O God, Thou God of my salvation; my tongue shall rejoice in Thy righteousness. O Lord, Thou shalt open my lips, and my mouth shall declare Thy praise. For if Thou hadst desired sacrifice, I had given it; with whole-burnt offerings Thou shalt not be pleased. A sacrifice unto God is a broken spirit; a heart that is broken and humbled God will not despise. Do good, O Lord, in Thy good pleasure unto Sion, and let the walls of Jerusalem be builded. Then shalt Thou be pleased with sacrifice of right-eousness, with oblation and whole-burnt offerings. Then shall they offer bullocks upon Thine altar.

And immediately:

The Canon for Holy Communion
Second Tone
ODE I

Eirmos: Come, O ye people, let us sing a hymn to Christ our God, Who divided the sea and guided the people whom He brought out of the bondage of Egypt, for He is glorified.

Refrain: Create in me a clean heart, O God, and renew a right spirit within me.

May Thy holy Body be unto me the Bread of life eternal, O compassionate Lord, and Thy precious Blood be also the healing of many forms of illness.

Refrain: Cast me not away from Thy presence, and take not Thy Holy Spirit from me.

Defiled by unseemly deeds, I the

wretched one am unworthy, O Christ, of the communion of Thy most pure Body and divine Blood, which do Thou vouchsafe me.

Glory to the Father, and to the Son, and to the Holy Spirit, both now and ever, and unto the ages of ages. Amen.

O blessed Bride of God, O good soil that grew the Corn untilled and saving to the world, vouchsafe me to be saved by eating it.

ODE III

Eirmos: By establishing me on the rock of faith, Thou hast enlarged my mouth over mine enemies, for my spirit rejoiceth when I sing: There is none holy as our God, and none righteous beside Thee, O Lord.

Create in me a clean heart, O God, and renew a right spirit within me.

Teardrops grant me, O Christ, to cleanse my defiled heart, that, purified and with a good conscience, I may come with faith and fear, O Master, to the communion of Thy divine Gifts.

Cast me not away from Thy presence, and take not Thy Holy Spirit from me.

May Thy most pure Body and divine Blood be unto me for remission of sins, for communion with the Holy Spirit, and unto life eternal, O Lover of mankind, and to the estrangement of passions and sorrows.

Glory to the Father, and to the Son, and to the Holy Spirit, both now and ever, and unto the ages of ages. Amen.

O thou most holy table of the Bread of Life that for mercy's sake came down from on high, giving new life to the world, vouchsafe even me, the unworthy, to eat it with fear, and live.

ODE IV

Eirmos: From a Virgin didst Thou come, not as an ambassador nor as an angel, but the very Lord Himself incarnate, and didst save me, the whole man. Wherefore, I cry to Thee: Glory to Thy power, O Lord.

Create in me a clean heart, O God, and renew a right spirit within me.

O Thou Who wast incarnate for our sake, O Most-merciful One, Thou didst will to be slain as a sheep for the sin of mankind. Wherefore, I entreat Thee to blot out my sins also.

Cast me not away from Thy presence, and take not Thy Holy Spirit from me.

Heal the wounds of my soul, O Lord, and sanctify all of me, and vouchsafe, O Master, that I the wretched one may partake of Thy divine Mystical Supper.

Glory to the Father, and to the Son, and to the Holy Spirit, both now and ever, and unto the ages of ages. Amen.

Propitiate for me also Him that came from thy womb, O Lady, and keep me, thy servant, undefiled and blameless, so that by obtaining the spiritual Pearl I may be sanctified.

ODE V

Eirmos: O Lord, Give of light and Creator of the ages, guide us in the light of Thy commandments, for we know none other God beside Thee.

Create in me a clean heart, O God, and renew a right spirit within me.

As Thou didst foretell, O Christ, so let it be unto Thy wicked servant, and in me abide, as Thou didst promise; for behold, I eat Thy divine Body and drink Thy Blood.

Cast me not away from Thy presence, and take not Thy Holy Spirit from me.

O Word of God and God, may the live coal of Thy Body be unto the enlightenment of me who am in darkness, and Thy Blood unto the cleansing of my defiled soul.

Glory to the Father, and to the Son, and to the Holy Spirit, both now and ever, and unto the ages of ages. Amen.

O Mary, Mother of God, precious tabernacle of fragrance, through thy prayers make me a chosen vessel, that I may partake of the Sacrament of thy Son.

ODE VI

Eirmos: Whirled about in the abyss of sin,

I appeal to the unfathomable abyss of Thy compassion: From corruption raise me up, O God.

Create in me a clean heart, O God, and renew a right spirit within me.

O Saviour, sanctify my mind, my soul, my heart, and my body, and vouchsafe me uncondemned, O Master, to approach the fearful Mysteries.

Cast me not away from Thy presence, and take not Thy Holy Spirit from me.

Grant that I may be rid of passions, and have the assistance of Thy grace, and strengthening of life by the communion of Thy Holy Mysteries, O Christ.

Glory to the Father, and to the Son, and to the Holy Spirit, both now and ever, and unto the ages of ages. Amen.

O Holy Word of God and God, sanctify all of me as I now come to Thy divine Mysteries, through the prayers of Thy holy Mother.

Lord, have mercy. *Thrice.*

Glory to the Father, and to the Son, and to the Holy Spirit, both now and ever, and unto the ages of ages. Amen.

Kontakion, Second Tone: Count me not unworthy, O Christ, to receive now the Bread which is Thy Body, and Thy divine Blood, and to partake, O Master, of Thy most pure and dread Mysteries, wretched though I be. Let these not be for me unto judgment, but unto life immortal and everlasting.

ODE VII

Eirmos: The wise children did not serve the golden image, but went themselves into the flame and reviled the pagan gods. They cried in the midst of the flame, and the angel bedewed them: Already the prayer of your lips was heard.

Create in me a clean heart, O God, and renew a right spirit within me.

May the communion of Thine immortal Mysteries, the source of blessings, O Christ, be to me now light, and life, and dispassion, and for progress and increase in the most divine virtues, O only Good One, that I may glorify Thee.

Cast me not away from Thy presence, and take not Thy Holy Spirit from me.

That I may be delivered from passions, and enemies, need, and every sorrow, I now draw nigh with trembling, love, and reverence, O Lover of mankind, to Thine immortal and divine Mysteries. Vouchsafe me to hymn Thee: Blessed art Thou, O Lord God of our fathers.

Glory to the Father, and to the Son, and to the Holy Spirit, both now and ever, and unto the ages of ages. Amen.

O thou who art full of grace, who beyond understanding gavest birth to Christ the Saviour, I thy servant, the impure, now entreat thee, the pure: Cleanse me, who am now about to approach the most pure Mysteries, from all defilement of flesh and spirit.

ODE VIII

Eirmos: God Who descended into the fiery furnace unto the Hebrew children, and changed the flame into dew, praise Him as

Lord, O ye works, and supremely exalt Him unto all ages.

Create in me a clean heart, O God, and renew a right spirit within me.

Of Thy heavenly and dread holy Mysteries, O Christ, and of Thy divine Mystical Supper vouchsafe now even me, the despairing one, to partake, O God my Saviour.

Cast me not away from Thy presence, and take not Thy Holy Spirit from me.

Fleeing for refuge to Thy loving-kindness, O Good One, with fear I cry unto Thee: Abide in me, O Saviour, and I, as Thou hast said, in Thee. For behold, presuming on Thy mercy, I eat Thy Body and drink Thy Blood.

Glory to the Father, and to the Son, and to the Holy Spirit, both now and ever, and unto the ages of ages. Amen.

I tremble at taking fire, lest I be consumed as wax and grass. O fearful Mystery! O the loving-kindness of God! How is it that I, being but clay, partake of the divine Body and Blood, and am made incorruptible?

ODE IX

Eirmos: The Son of the unoriginate Father, God, and Lord, hath appeared unto us incarnate of the Virgin, to enlighten those in darkness and to gather the dispersed. Wherefore, the all-hymned Theotokos do we magnify.

Create in me a clean heart, O God, and renew a right spirit within me.

Christ It is, O taste and see! The Lord for our sake made like unto us of old, once offered Himself as an offering to His Father, and is ever slain, sanctifying them that partake.

Cast me not away from Thy presence, and take not Thy Holy Spirit from me.

May I be sanctified in soul and body, O Master, may I be enlightened, may I be saved, may I become Thy dwelling through the communion of Thy holy Mysteries, having Thee with the Father and the Spirit living in me, O

Benefactor plenteous in mercy.

Glory to the Father, and to the Son, and to the Holy Spirit.

May Thy Body and Thy most precious Blood, O my Saviour, be unto me as fire and light, consuming the substance of sin, and burning the thorns of passions, and enlightening all of me to worship Thy Divinity.

Both now and ever, and unto the ages of ages. Amen.

God took flesh of thy pure blood; wherefore, all generations do hymn thee, O Lady, and throngs of heavenly minds glorify thee, for through thee they have clearly seen Him Who ruleth all things endued with human nature.

And immediately: It is truly meet ... *Trisagion.* O Most Holy Trinity... Our Father...*And the troparion of the day, if it be the feast of the Lord's Nativity. If it be Sunday, the Sunday troparion of the tone. If not, these:*

Sixth Tone: Have mercy on us, O Lord, have mercy on us; for at a loss for any defence, this prayer do we sinners offer unto Thee as Master: have mercy on us.

Glory to the Father, and to the Son, and to the Holy Spirit.

Lord, have mercy on us, for we have hoped in Thee, be not angry with us greatly, neither remember our iniquities; but look upon us now as Thou art compassionate, and deliver us from our enemies; for Thou art our God, and we, Thy people; all are the works of Thy hands, and we call upon Thy name.

Both now and ever, and unto the ages of ages. Amen.

The door of compassion open unto us, O blessed Theotokos, for, hoping in thee, let us not perish; through thee may we be delivered from adversities, for thou art the salvation of the Christian race.

Then: Lord, have mercy. *Forty times.*

And reverences [bows, prostrations], as many as thou desirest.

And thereafter these lines:

If thou desirest, O man, to eat the Body of
the Master,

Approach with fear, lest thou be burnt:
for It is fire.

And when thou drinkest the Divine Blood
unto communion,

First be reconciled to them that have
grieved thee,

Then dare to eat the Mystical Food.

Other lines:

Before partaking of the awesome Sacrifice

Of the life-giving Body of the Master,

After this manner pray with trembling.

A Prayer of Basil the Great, 1:

O Master Lord Jesus Christ our God, Source of life and immortality, Creator of all things visible and invisible, the co-eternal and co-unoriginate Son of the unoriginate Father, Who out of Thy great goodness, didst in the latter days clothe Thyself in flesh, and wast crucified, and buried

for us ungrateful and evil-disposed
ones, and hast renewed with Thine
Own Blood our nature corrupted by
sin: Do Thou Thyself, O Immortal
King, accept the repentance of me a
sinner, and incline Thine ear to me,
and hearken unto my words. For I
have sinned against heaven and before
Thee, and I am not worthy to look
upon the height of Thy glory; for I
have angered Thy goodness by trans-
gressing Thy commandments and not
obeying Thine injunctions. But Thou,
O Lord, Who art not vengeful, but long-
suffering and plenteous in mercy, hast
not given me over to be destroyed with
my sins, but always Thou awaitest my
complete conversion. For Thou hast
said, O Lover of mankind, through Thy
prophet: For I desire not the death of
the sinner, but that he should return
and live. For Thou desirest not, O

Master, to destroy the work of Thy
hands, neither shalt Thou be pleased
with the destruction of men, but
desirest that all be saved and come to a
knowledge of the truth. Wherefore,
even I, although unworthy of heaven
and earth, and of this temporal life,
having submitted my whole self to sin,
and made myself a slave of pleasure,
and having defaced Thine image, yet
being Thy work and creation, wretched
though I be, I despair not of my salvation, and dare to approach Thine immeasurable loving-kindness. Accept,
then, even me, O Lord, Lover of mankind, as Thou didst accept the sinful
woman, the thief, the publican and the
prodigal; and take away the heavy burden of my sins, Thou that takest away
the sin of the world, and healest the
infirmities of mankind; Who callest the
weary and heavy-laden unto Thyself

and givest them rest, Who camest not
to call the righteous, but sinners to
repentance. And do Thou cleanse me
from all defilement of flesh and spirit,
and teach me to achieve holiness in
fear of Thee; that with the pure testimony of my conscience, receiving a
portion of Thy Holy Things, I may be
united unto Thy holy Body and Blood,
and have Thee living and abiding in
me with the Father and Thy Holy
Spirit. Yea, O Lord Jesus Christ my God,
let not the communion of Thine
immaculate and life-giving Mysteries
be unto me for judgment, neither unto
infirmity of soul and body because of
my partaking of them unworthily; but
grant me until my last breath to receive
without condemnation the portion of
Thy Holy Things, unto communion
with the Holy Spirit, as a provision for
life eternal, for an acceptable defence

at Thy dread judgment seat; so that I also, with all Thine elect, may become a partaker of Thine incorruptible blessings, which Thou hast prepared for them that love Thee, O Lord, in whom Thou art glorified unto the ages. Amen.

A Prayer of Our Father among the Saints, John Chrysostom, 2:

O Lord my God, I know that I am not worthy nor sufficient that Thou shouldest enter beneath the roof of the temple of my soul, for all is empty and fallen, and Thou hast not in me a place worthy to lay Thy head; but as from on high Thou didst humble Thyself for our sake, do Thou now also lower Thyself to my lowliness; and as Thou didst consent to lie in a cave and in a manger of dumb beasts, so consent also to lie in the manger of mine irrational soul, and to enter into my defiled body. And as Thou didst not refuse to enter and to dine with sinners in the house of Simon the Leper, so deign also to enter into the house of my lowly soul, leprous and sinful. And as Thou didst not reject the harlot and sinner like me, when she came and touched Thee, so be compassionate also with me a sinner, as I approach and touch Thee. And as Thou didst feel no loathing for the defiled and unclean lips of her that kissed Thee, do Thou also not loathe my defiled lips nor mine abominable and impure mouth, and my polluted and unclean tongue. But let the fiery coal of Thy most holy Body and Thy precious Blood be unto me for sanctification and enlightenment, and health for my lowly soul and body, unto the lightening of the burden of my many sins, for preservation from every act of the devil, for the expulsion and prohibition of mine evil and wicked habits, unto the mortification of the passions, unto the keeping of Thy commandments, unto the application of Thy divine grace, unto the acquiring of Thy kingdom. For not with disdain do I approach Thee, O Christ God, but as one trusting in Thine ineffable goodness, and that I may not by much abstaining from Thy communion become the prey of the spiritual wolf. Wherefore do I entreat Thee, for Thou art the only Holy One, O Master: sanctify my soul and body, my mind and heart, my belly and inward parts, and renew me entirely. And implant Thy fear in my members, and make Thy sanctification inalienable from me, and be unto me a helper and defender, guiding my life in peace, vouchsafing me also to stand at Thy right hand

with Thy saints, through the intercessions and supplications of Thy most
pure Mother, of Thine immaterial
ministers and immaculate hosts, and of
all the saints who from the ages have
been pleasing unto Thee. Amen.

Another Prayer, of Symeon Metaphrastes, 3:

O only pure and sinless Lord, Who
through the ineffable compassion of Thy love for mankind didst take
on all of our substance from the pure
and virgin blood of her that bare Thee
supernaturally through the descent of
the Divine Spirit and the good will of
the everlasting Father; O Christ Jesus,
Wisdom of God, and Peace, and
Power, Thou Who through the
assumption of our nature didst take
upon Thyself Thy life-giving and saving
Passion — the Cross, the nails, the
spear, and death: mortify the soul-cor-

rupting passions of my body. Thou Who by Thy burial didst lead captive the kingdom of hades, bury with good thoughts mine evil schemes, and destroy the spirits of evil. Thou Who by Thy life-bearing Resurrection on the third day didst raise up our fallen forefather, raise me up who have slipped down into sin, setting before me the ways of repentance. Thou Who by Thy most glorious Ascension didst deify the flesh that Thou hadst taken, and didst honour it with a seat at the right hand of the Father, vouchsafe me through partaking of Thy holy Mysteries to obtain a place at Thy right hand among them that are saved. O Thou Who by the descent of Thy Spirit, the Comforter, didst make Thy holy disciples worthy vessels, show me also to be a receptacle of His coming. Thou Who art to come again to judge the world in righteousness, deign to let me also meet Thee on the clouds, my Judge and Creator, with all Thy saints; that I may endlessly glorify and praise Thee, with Thine unoriginate Father, and Thy Most-holy and good and life-creating Spirit, now and ever, and unto the ages of ages. Amen.

Of the divine Damascene, 4:

O Master Lord Jesus Christ our God, Who alone hast authority to remit the sins of men: Do Thou, as the Good One and Lover of mankind, overlook all mine offences, whether committed with knowledge or in ignorance. And vouchsafe me to partake without condemnation of Thy Divine, glorious, immaculate, and life-giving Mysteries; not as a burden, nor for punishment, nor for an increase of sins, but unto purification and sanctification, and as a pledge of the life and kingdom to come, as a bulwark and help, and for the destruction of enemies, and for the blotting out of my many transgressions. For Thou art a God of mercy, and compassion, and love for mankind, and unto Thee do we send up glory, with the Father, and the Holy Spirit, now and ever, and unto the ages of ages. Amen.

Of Basil the Great, 5:

I know, O Lord, that I partake un-worthily of Thine immaculate Body and Thy precious Blood, and that I am guilty, and eat and drink damnation to myself, not discerning the Body and Blood of Thee, my Christ and God; but taking courage from Thy compassion I approach Thee Who hast said: He that eateth My Flesh, and drinketh My Blood, abideth in Me, and I in him. Show compassion, therefore, O Lord, and do not accuse me, a sinner, but deal with me according to Thy mercy; and let these Holy Things be for me unto healing, and purification, and enlightenment, and preservation, and salvation, and unto sanctification of soul and body; unto the driving away of every phantasy, and evil practice, and activity of the devil working mentally in my members; unto confidence and love toward Thee, unto correction of life, unto steadfastness, unto an increase of virtue and perfection, unto fulfillment of the commandments, unto communion with the Holy Spirit, as a provision for life eternal, as an acceptable defence at Thy dread tribunal, not unto judgment or condemnation.

A Prayer of Saint Symeon the New Theologian, 6:

From sullied lips, from an abominable heart, from a tongue impure, from a soul defiled, accept my supplication, O my Christ, and disdain me not, neither my words, nor my ways, nor my shamelessness. Grant me to say boldly that which I desire, O my Christ. Or rather, teach me what I ought to do and say. I have sinned more than the sinful woman who, having learned where Thou wast lodging, bought myrrh, and came daringly to anoint Thy feet, my God, my Master, and my Christ. As Thou didst not reject her when she drew near from her heart, neither, O Word, be Thou filled with loathing for me, but grant me Thy feet to clasp and kiss, and with floods of tears, as with most precious myrrh, dare to anoint them. Wash me with my tears, and purify me with them, O Word; remit also my transgressions, and grant me pardon. Thou knowest the multitude of mine evils,

Thou knowest also my sores, and Thou seest my wounds; but also Thou knowest my faith, and Thou beholdest my good intentions, and Thou hearest my sighs. Nothing is hidden from Thee, my God, my Creator, My Redeemer, neither a teardrop, nor a part of a drop. My deeds not yet done Thine eyes have seen, and in Thy book even things not yet accomplished are written by Thee. See my lowliness, see my toil, how great it is, and all my sins take from me, O God of all; that with a pure heart, a trembling mind, and a contrite soul I may partake of Thy spotless and most holy Mysteries, by which all that eat and drink in purity of heart are quickened and deified. For Thou, O my Master, hast said: Everyone that eateth My Flesh and drinketh My Blood abideth in Me, and I in him. True is every word of my Master and God; for whosoever partaketh of the divine and deifying grace is no more alone, but with Thee, my Christ, the three-sunned Light that enlighteneth the world. And that I may not remain alone without Thee, the Life-giver, my Breath, my Life, my Rejoicing, the Salvation of the world, therefore have I drawn nigh unto Thee, as Thou seest, with tears, and with a contrite soul. O Ransom of mine offences, I ask Thee to receive me, and that I may partake without condemnation of Thy life-giving and perfect Mysteries, that Thou mayest remain, as Thou hast said, with me, a thrice-wretched one, lest the deceiver, finding me without Thy grace, craftily seize me, and having beguiled me, draw me away from Thy deifying words. Wherefore, I fall down before Thee, and fervently cry unto Thee: As Thou didst receive the prodigal, and the sinful woman who drew near, so receive me, the prodigal and profligate, O Compassionate One. With contrite soul I now come to Thee. I know, O Saviour, that none other hath sinned against Thee as have I, nor hath wrought the deeds that I have done. But this again I know, that neither the magnitude of mine offences nor the multitude of my sins surpasseth the abundant long-suffering of my God and His exceeding love for mankind; but with sympathetic mercy Thou dost purify and illumine them that fervently repent, and makest them partakers of the light, sharers of Thy divinity without stint. And, strange to angels and to the minds of men, Thou conversest with them oftimes, as with Thy true friends. These things make me bold, these things give me wings, O Christ. And taking courage from the wealth of Thy benefactions to us, rejoicing and trembling at once, I partake of Fire, I that am grass. And, strange wonder! I am bedewed without being consumed, as the bush of old burned without being consumed. Now with thankful mind, and grateful heart, with thankfulness in my members, my soul and body, I worship and magnify and glorify Thee, my God, for blessed art Thou, both now and unto the ages.

Another Prayer of Chrysostom, 7:

O God, loose, remit, and pardon me my transgressions wherein I have sinned against Thee, whether by word, deed, or thought, voluntarily or involuntarily, consciously or unconsciously; forgive me all, for Thou art good and the Lover of mankind. And through the intercessions of Thy most pure Mother, Thy noetic ministers and holy hosts, and all the saints who from the ages have been pleasing unto Thee, deign to allow me without condemnation Thy holy and immacluate Body and precious Blood, unto the healing of soul and body, and unto the purification of mine evil thoughts. For Thine is the kingdom, and the power, and the glory, with the Father and the Holy Spirit, now and ever, and unto the ages of ages. Amen.

Of the same, 8:

I am not sufficient, O Master and Lord, that Thou shouldst enter under the roof of my soul; but as Thou dost will as the Lover of mankind to dwell in me, I dare to approach Thee. Thou commandest: I shall open the doors which Thou alone didst create, that Thou mayest enter with Thy love for mankind, as is Thy nature, that Thou mayest enter and enlighten my darkened thought. I believe that Thou wilt do this, for Thou didst not drive away the sinful woman when she came unto Thee with tears, neither didst Thou reject the publican who repented, nor didst Thou spurn the thief who acknowledged Thy kingdom, nor didst Thou leave the repentant persecutor to himself; but all of them that came unto Thee in repentance Thou didst number among Thy friends, O Thou Who alone art blessed, always, now and unto endless ages. Amen.

Of the same, 9:

O Lord Jesus Christ my God, loose, remit, cleanse, and forgive me, Thy sinful and unprofitable, and unworthy servant, my transgressions and offences and fallings into sin, which I have committed against Thee from my youth until the present day and hour, whether consciously or unconsciously, whether by words or deeds, or in thought or imagination, in habit, and in all my senses. And through the intercessions of her that seedlessly gave Thee birth, the most pure and Ever-Virgin Mary, Thy Mother, the only hope that maketh not ashamed, and my mediation and salvation, vouchsafe me without condemnation to partake of Thine immaculate, immortal, life-giving, and awesome Mysteries, unto the remission of sins and for life eternal, unto sanctification and enlightenment, strength, healing, and health of both soul and body, and unto the consumption and complete destruction of mine evil reasonings and intentions and prejudices and nocturnal phantasies of dark and evil spirits; for Thine is the kingdom, and the power, and the glory, and the honour, and the worship, with the Father and Thy Holy

Spirit, now and ever, and unto the ages of ages. Amen.

Another Prayer of John Damascene, 10:

I stand before the doors of Thy temple, yet I do not put away evil thoughts. But do Thou, O Christ God, Who didst justify the publican, and didst have mercy on the woman of Canaan, and didst open the doors of paradise to the thief, open unto me the abyss of Thy love for mankind, and receive me as I come and touch Thee, as Thou didst receive the sinful woman and the woman with an issue of blood. For the one received healing easily by touching the hem of Thy garment, while the other, by clasping Thy most pure feet, carried away absolution of sins. And I, a wretch, daring to receive Thy whole Body, let me not be consumed by fire; but receive me, as Thou didst receive them, and enlighten my spiritual senses, burning up my sinful errors; through the intercessions of her that seedlessly gave Thee birth, and of the heavenly hosts, for blessed art Thou unto the ages of ages. Amen.

Another Prayer of Chrysostom:

I believe, O Lord, and I confess that Thou art truly the Christ, the Son of the living God, Who came into the world to save sinners, of whom I am chief. Moreover, I believe that this is truly Thy most pure Body, and this is truly Thine Own precious Blood; wherefore, I pray Thee: Have mercy on me and forgive me my transgressions, voluntary and involuntary, whether in word or deed, in knowledge or in ignorance. And vouchsafe me to partake without condemnation of Thy most pure Mysteries, unto the remission of sins and life everlasting. Amen.

When coming to partake, say to thyself these lines of Metaphrastes:

Behold, I approach the Divine Communion.

O Creator, let me not be burnt by communicating,

For Thou art Fire, consuming the unworthy.

But, rather, purify me of all impurity.

Then again say:

Of Thy Mystical Supper, O Son of God, receive me today as a communicant; for I will not speak of the Mystery to Thine enemies; nor will I give Thee a kiss, as did Judas, but like the thief do I confess Thee: Remember me, O Lord, in Thy kingdom.

Furthermore, these lines:

Be awe-stricken, O mortal, beholding the deifying Blood;

For It is a fire that consumeth the unworthy.

The Divine Body both deifieth and nourisheth me.

It deifieth the spirit, and wondrously nourisheth the mind.

Then the Troparia:

Thou hast sweetened me with Thy love, O Christ, and by Thy Divine zeal hast Thou changed me. But do Thou consume my sins with immaterial fire, and vouchsafe me to be filled with delight in Thee; that, leaping for joy, O Good One, I may magnify Thy two comings.

Into the brilliant company of Thy saints how shall I the unworthy enter? For if I dare to enter into the bridechamber, my garment betrayeth me, for it is not a wedding garment, and I shall be bound and cast out by the angels. Cleanse, O Lord, my soul of pollution, and save me, as Thou art the Lover of mankind.

Then the Prayer:

O Master, Lover of mankind, O Lord Jesus Christ my God, let not these Holy Things be unto me for judgment, through my being unworthy, but unto the purification and sanctification of soul and body, and as a pledge of the life and kingdom to come. For it is good for me to cleave unto God, to put my hope of salvation in the Lord.

And again:

Of Thy Mystical Supper, O Son of God, receive me today as a communicant; for I will not speak of the Mystery to Thine enemies; nor will I give Thee a kiss, as did Judas, but like the thief do I confess Thee: Remember me, O Lord, in Thy kingdom.

THE PRAYERS
AFTER HOLY COMMUNION

When thou hast received the good Communion of the life-giving Mystical Gifts, give praise immediately, give thanks greatly, and from the soul say fervently unto God these things:

Glory to Thee, O God.
Glory to Thee, O God.
Glory to Thee, O God.

Then this **Prayer of Thanksgiving:**

I thank Thee, O Lord my God, that Thou hast not rejected me, a sinner, but hast vouchsafed me to be a communicant of Thy Holy Things. I thank Thee that Thou hast vouchsafed me, the unworthy, to partake of Thy most pure and heavenly Gifts. But, O

Master, Lover of mankind, Who for our sake didst die and didst rise again, and didst bestow upon us these dread and life-giving Mysteries for the well-being and sanctification of our souls and bodies, grant that these may be even unto me for the healing of both soul and body, for the averting of everything hostile, for the enlightenment of the eyes of my heart, for the peace of the powers of my soul, for faith unashamed, for love unfeigned, for the fullness of wisdom, for the keeping of Thy commandments, for an increase of Thy Divine grace, and for the attainment of Thy kingdom; that being preserved by them in Thy holiness, I may always remember Thy grace, and no longer live for myself, but for Thee our Master and Benefactor; and thus when I shall have departed this life in hope of life eternal, I may attain unto everlasting rest, where the sound of them that keep festival is unceasing, and the delight is endless of them that behold the ineffable beauty of Thy countenance. For Thou art the true desire and the unutterable gladness of them that love Thee, O Christ our God, and all creation doth hymn Thee unto the ages. Amen.

Of Basil the Great, 2:

O Master Christ God, King of the ages, and Creator of all things, I thank Thee for all the good things which Thou hast bestowed upon me, and for the Communion of Thy most pure and life-giving Mysteries. I pray Thee, therefore, O Good One and Lover of Mankind: Keep me under Thy protection and in the shadow of Thy wings and grant me, even until my last breath, to partake worthily, with a pure conscience, of Thy Holy Things, unto the remission of sins and life eternal. For Thou art the Bread of Life, the Source of holiness, the Giver of good things; and unto Thee do we send up glory, together with the Father and the Holy Spirit, now and ever, and unto the ages of ages. Amen.

Verses of Metaphrastes, 3:

O Thou who givest me willingly Thy Flesh as food, Thou Who art Fire that doth consume the unworthy, burn me not, O my Creator; but, rather, enter Thou into my members, into all my joints, my reins, my heart. Burn up the thorns of all my sins. Purify my soul, sanctify my thoughts. Strengthen my substance together with my bones. Enlighten my simple five senses. Nail down the whole of me with Thy fear. Ever protect, preserve, and keep me from every soul-corrupting deed and word. Purify and cleanse, and adorn me; make me comely, give me under-standing, and enlighten me. Show me to be the dwelling-place of Thy Spirit alone, and no longer the habitation of sin; that from me as Thine abode through the entry of Communion, every evildoer, every passion, may flee as from fire. As intercessors I offer unto Thee all the saints, the command-ers of the bodiless hosts, Thy Forerunner, the wise apostles, and fur-ther, Thine undefiled pure Mother, whose entreaties do Thou accept, O my compassionate Christ, and make Thy servant a child of light. For Thou alone art our sanctification, O Good One, and the radiance of our souls, and unto Thee as God and Master, we all send up glory, as is meet, every day.

Another Prayer:

O Lord Jesus Christ our God, may Thy holy Body be unto me for life eternal, and Thy precious Blood for the remission of sins; and may this Eucharist be unto me for joy, health, and gladness. And at Thy dread Second Coming vouchsafe me, a sinner, to stand at the right hand of Thy glory, through the intercessions of Thy most pure Mother and of all the saints.

Another Prayer,
to the Most Holy Theotokos:

O most holy Lady Theotokos, light of my darkened soul, my hope, protection, refuge, consolation, my joy: I thank thee that thou hast vouchsafed me, who am unworthy, to be a partaker of the most pure Body and precious Blood of thy Son. O thou who gavest birth to the True Light, do thou enlighten the spiritual eyes of my heart; thou who gavest birth to the Source of immortality, revive me who am dead in sin; thou who art the lovingly-compassionate Mother of the merciful God, have mercy on me, and grant me compunction, and contrition in my heart, and humility in my thoughts, and the recall of my thoughts from captivity. And vouchsafe me until my last breath to receive without condemnation the sanctification of the most pure Mysteries, for the healing of both soul and body; and grant me tears of repentance and confession, that I may hymn and glorify thee all the days of my life, for blessed and most glorious art thou unto the ages. Amen.

Then: Now lettest Thou Thy servant depart in peace, O Master, according to Thy word; for mine eyes have seen Thy salvation which Thou hast prepared before the face of all peoples, a light of revelation for the Gentiles, and the glory of Thy people Israel.

Holy God, Holy Mighty, Holy Immortal, have mercy on us. *Thrice.*

Glory to the Father, and to the Son, and to the Holy Spirit, both now and ever, and unto the ages of ages. Amen.

O Most Holy Trinity, have mercy on us. O Lord, blot out our sins. O Master, pardon our iniquities. O Holy One, visit and heal our infirmities for Thy name's sake.

Lord, have mercy. *Thrice.*

Glory to the Father, and to the Son, and to the Holy Spirit, both now and ever, and unto the ages of ages. Amen.

Our Father, Who art in the heavens, hallowed be Thy name. Thy kingdom come, Thy will be done, on earth as it is in heaven. Give us this day our daily bread, and forgive us our debts, as we forgive our debtors; and lead us not into temptation, but deliver us from the evil one.

Troparion to Saint John Chrysostom, Eighth Tone:

Grace shining forth from thy mouth like a beacon hath illumined the universe, and disclosed to the world treasures of uncovetousness, and shown us the heights of humility; but while instructing by thy words, O Father John Chrysostom, intercede with the Word, Christ our God, to save our souls.

Glory to the Father, and to the Son, and to the Holy Spirit.

Kontakion, Sixth Tone:

From the heavens hast thou received divine grace and by thy lips thou dost teach all to worship the One God in Trinity, O John Chrysostom, all-blessed righteous one. Rightly do we acclaim thee, for thou art a teacher revealing things divine.

Both now and ever, and unto the ages of ages. Amen.

O protection of Christians that cannot be put to shame, O mediation unto the Creator unfailing, disdain not the suppliant voices of sinners; but be thou quick, O good one, to help us who in faith cry unto thee; hasten to intercession and speed thou to make supplication, thou who dost ever protect, O Theotokos, them that honour thee.

But if it be the Liturgy of St. Basil, read the:

Troparion to Saint Basil the Great, First Tone:

Thy fame hath gone forth into all the earth, which hath received thy word. Thereby thou hast divinely taught the Faith; thou hast made manifest the nature of created things; thou hast made the moral life of men a royal priesthood. O Basil our righteous father, intercede with Christ God that our souls be saved.

Glory to the Father, and to the Son, and to the Holy Spirit.

Kontakion, Fourth Tone:

Thou didst prove to be an unshakable foundation of the Church, giving to all mortals an inviolate lordship, and sealing it with thy doctrines, O righteous Basil, revealer of heavenly things.

Both now... O protection of Christians....*(page 385).*

But if it be the Liturgy of the Presanctified Gifts:

Troparion to Saint Gregory the Dialogist, Fourth Tone:

Thou who hast received of God divine grace from on high, O glorious Gregory, and hast been fortified by His power, thou didst will to walk according to the Gospel; wherefore, thou hast received of Christ the reward of thy labours, O all-blessed one. Entreat Him that He save our souls.

Glory to the Father, and to the Son, and to the Holy Spirit.

Kontakion, Third Tone:

Thou hast shown thyself to be a leader like unto the Chief Shepherd Christ, O Father Gregory, guiding flocks of monks into the heavenly sheepfold, and from whence thou didst teach the flock of Christ His commandments. And now thou dost rejoice with them and dance in the heavenly mansions.

Both now....O protection of Christians....*(page 385).*

Lord, have mercy. *Twelve times.*

Glory. Both now.

More honourable than the Cherubim, and beyond compare more glorious than the Seraphim, who without corruption gavest birth to God the Word, the very Theotokos, thee do we magnify.

And the Dismissal.

HOW ONE SHOULD PRAY IN CHURCH

Orthodox Christians have received from the Holy Fathers and observe the following practice throughout the world:

1. Entering the holy temple and making the sign of the Cross upon oneself thrice, one makes a bow with each, saying:

"Thou hast created me, O Lord, have mercy on me."

"O God, be merciful to me a sinner."

"Countless times have I sinned, O Lord, forgive me.

2. Then, having bowed to the right and the left, one stands in one's place and listens to the psalms and prayers read in church, but one does not say to oneself other prayers of one's own choosing nor read them according to books different from the church chanting, for such things the holy Apostle Paul condemns as having forsaken the assembly of the Church (Hebrews 10:25).

3.   Prostrations and bows should not be made according to one's inclination, but according to the regulations of the holy apostles and holy fathers, namely: at the reading of the Trisagion ("Holy God,"), "O come let us worship," and the threefold "Alleluia," one makes upon himself the sign of the Cross thrice, concluding with bows; likewise also at the reading: "Vouchsafe, O Lord," as well as at the beginning of the Great Doxology ("Glory to God in the highest,"), and after the words of the priest: "Glory to Thee, O Christ God, our hope."   After each exclamation of the priest, and also at the reading by the reader of: "More honourable than the Cherubim," one makes the sign of the Cross and a bow.

On weekdays prostrations are made at the *Liturgy:*

    a) at the beginning of the chanting of "It is meet and right";

    b) when the prayer "We praise Thee" is finished;

    c) at the end of the prayer: "It is truly meet," or its substitute megalynarion;

    d) at the beginning of the prayer "Our Father";

    e) at the bringing forth of the Holy Gifts

for Communion;

f) and at the words "Always, now and ever."

At *Matins* or *Vigil,* when "The Theotokos and Mother of the Light let us magnify in song" is exclaimed, we make a prostration.

4. On *Sundays,* and likewise *from the day of Holy Pascha until Vespers on the day of Pentecost* (i.e., the "Kneeling Service"), and also *from the day of the Nativity of Christ until Theophany,* and likewise on the *day of Transfiguration* and on the *Exaltation* (except before the Cross), the Holy Apostles *utterly forbid kneeling and prostrations,* concerning which St. Basil the Great testified in a letter to the Blessed Amphilochius. Thus also the First and Sixth Ecumenical Councils established; for Sundays and other feasts of the Lord serve as reminders of our adoption by God, according to the word of the Apostle: "Wherefore thou art no more a servant, but a son" (Gal.4:7); for it is not proper for sons to make servile adoration.

5. Customarily, Orthodox Christians do not kneel, heads upright, but at the words of the priest (or deacon): "Again and again, on bended knee," and the rest, they bow the face to the ground; the custom of kneeling at will, folding the arms, and beating oneself on the

breast comes from the Western heretics, and in the Orthodox Church it is not allowed. Orthodox Christians, in accordance with the Church rule, make prostrations at the appointed times, bowing prone upon the ground and again standing on the feet.

6. In church, whenever the people are blessed with the Cross or the Gospel, with an icon or the chalice, they all make the sign of the Cross, bowing the head; but when blessed with candles, or the hand(s), or censed, Orthodox Christians ought not to make the sing of the Cross, but only bow the head. However, during the week of Holy Pascha when the priest censes with the Cross in his hand, then all make the sign of the Cross and answer: "Truly He is risen!" In this way ought we to distinguish between reverence toward holy things and toward persons, although they be of priestly rank.

7. When receiving a blessing from either a priest or a bishop, a Christian kisses the right hand of him who bestows the blessing, but does not make the sign of the Cross before doing so. It is not proper to kiss the left hand of clergy, for this is a Jewish usage, but the right hand with which the blessing is given.

8. According to the teaching of the Holy Fathers, the sign of the Cross should be made in the following manner: the thumb and first two fingers of the right hand are joined at their tips and the other fingers folded across the palm. We then touch the brow, the belly, and the right and left shoulders, and make a slight bow. Of those who sign themselves with all five fingers, or who bow before finishing the Cross, or simply wave their hand in the air or before their breast, Chrysostom says: "The demons rejoice at these mad gestures." On the other hand, the sign of the Cross, properly made with faith and reverence, terrifies the demons, calms sinful passions, and calls down divine grace.

RULES FOR BOWS AND
THE SIGN OF THE CROSS

The Sign of the Cross without Bows:

1. At the middle of the Six Psalms, at Alleluia, thrice.
2. At the beginning of the Creed.
3. At the dismissal: "May Christ our true God."
4. At the beginning of a reading from Holy Scripture: Gospel, Epistle, or Parable (at Vespers, Royal Hours).

The Sign of the Cross
with Bows from the Waist:

1. When entering or leaving a church — thrice.

2. At each petition of the ecteniae.

3. At each exclamation of the priest offering up glory to the Holy Trinity.

4. At the exclamations: "Take, eat"; "Drink of it, all of you"; "Thine Own of Thine Own"; and "Holy Things are for the holy."

5. At the words: "More honourable."

6. At each of the words:: "Let us worship," "Worship," "We fall down."

7. During the words: "Alleluia," "Holy God," "O come let us worship," and after the exclamation "Glory to Thee, O Christ God," before the dismissal — thrice.

8. At the canon, at the first and ninth odes, at the first refrain to the Lord, the Mother of God, or the saint.

9. After each sticheron (at which time the choir that has finished chanting makes the sign of the Cross).

10. At the Litia, after each of the first three petitions we sign ourselves and bow three times; after the remaining two petitions we sign ourselves and bow once.

The Sign of the Cross with Prostrations:

1. During fasts, on entering and leaving the church, thrice.

2. During fasts, after each refrain to the Song of the Theotokos, "Thee do we magnify."

3. At the beginning of the hymn: "It is meet and right to worship the Father."

4. After "We praise Thee."

5. After "It is truly meet," or its substitute megalynarion.

6. At the exclamation: "And vouchsafe us, O Master."

7. At the bringing forth of the Holy Gifts, at the words: "With fear of God," and the second time, at the words: "Always, now and ever."

8. During the Great Fast, at Great Compline, at the chanting of "O most holy Lady," at each verse; at the chanting of "O Theotokos and Virgin, rejoice," and the rest, at Great Lenten Vespers, three prostrations.

9. During fasts, at the prayer, "O Lord and Master of my life."

10 During fasts, at the concluding chanting: "Remember us, O Lord, when Thou comest in Thy kingdom,"—always three prostrations.

Bows from the Waist
without the Sign of the Cross:

1. At the words: "Peace be unto all."
2. "The blessing of the Lord be upon you."
3. "The grace of our Lord Jesus Christ."
4. "And may the mercies of our great God."
5. At the words of the deacon: "And unto the ages of ages" (after "For holy art Thou, O our God").

The Sign of the Cross is not to be made:

1. During psalms.
2. Generally while chanting.
3. During Ecteniae by the choir that chants the responses.

The making of the sign of the Cross and bows should be done *after* the chanting is finished, and not during the closing words.

Prostrations are not allowed:

On Sundays; from the Nativity of Christ through Theophany; from Pascha until Pentecost Sunday; on the day of Transfiguration; and on the Exaltation of the Cross (except three prostrations before the Cross).

Prostrations cease from the Entry at the Vespers of a feast, until "Vouchsafe, O Lord," at Vespers on the day of the feast itself.

THE ORDER FOR READING CANONS AND AKATHISTS WHEN ALONE

Before beginning any rule of prayer, and at its completion, the following reverences are made (prostrations or bows), which is called

The Seven-Bow Beginning.

1. O God, be merciful to me a sinner. *Bow.*

2. O God, cleanse me a sinner and have mercy on me. *Bow.*

3. Thou hast created me, O Lord, have mercy on me. *Bow.*

4. Countless times have I sinned, O Lord, forgive me. *Bow.*

5. My most holy Lady Theotokos, save me a sinner. *Bow.*

6. O Angel, my holy Guardian, protect me from all evil. *Bow.*

7. Holy Apostle (*or* Martyr, *or* Holy Father *N.*), pray to God for me. *Bow.*

Then: Through the prayers of our holy fathers, O Lord Jesus Christ our God, have mercy on us. Amen.

Glory to Thee, our God, glory to Thee.

O Heavenly King; Holy God (*thrice*); Glory, Both now; O Most Holy Trinity; Lord, have mercy (*thrice*); Glory, Both now; Our Father; Lord, have mercy (*twelve*); Glory, Both now; O come let us worship (*thrice*); Psalm 50, Have mercy on me, O God; I Believe; *and the reading of the canons and akathists.*

The Canons and Akathists are read as follows:

A. If one canon or akathist is to be read, it is read straight through.

B. If more than one canon is to be read, the first Ode of the first canon is read. If the refrain before the final or last two troparia is "Glory...Both now," the *Glory* is replaced by the refrain of the canon, and the *Both now* is replaced by "O most holy Theotokos, save us" (this comes before a *Theotokion,* a troparion to the Mother of God). Then the first Ode of the second canon is read, beginning with the refrain of the canon (the Eirmos being omitted since the Eirmos of the first canon only is read or chanted), etc. *Glory* and *Both now* are used as refrains only before the last two troparia (or the last troparion) of the final canon to be read. Then the third Ode of the first canon, beginning with the Eirmos, etc. After the third Ode: *Lord, have mercy (3), Glory, Both now,* and the Sessional Hymn(s). When there is more than one canon, the Kontakion of the second is read (and any additional ones are read) after the Sessional Hymns, and the *Glory...Both now* is read before the final two verses, not after *Lord, have mercy* as given above. Then Odes 4, 5, and 6 are read. After the Sixth Ode: *Lord, have mercy (3) Glory...Both now,* and the Kontakion of the first canon. Then Odes 7, 8, and 9 are read.

C. If an Akathist is read with the canon(s), it is inserted after the Sixth Ode. All Kontakia of the canon(s) are read after the Third Ode in this case.

After the Ninth Ode:

It is truly meet....

Trisagion through Our Father....

Have mercy on us, O Lord, have mercy on us...*and the rest of the Prayers before Sleep.*

If no other prayers are to be read, the closing is as follows:

It is truly meet...

The Prayer(s) following the canon(s).

Trisagion through Our Father...

Lord, have mercy, *thrice.*

Glory... Both now...

More honourable than the Cherubim....

Through the prayers of our holy fathers, O Lord Jesus Christ our God, have mercy on us. Amen.

Those who are preparing for Holy Communion are obliged to read three Canons and one Akathist the evening before. Usually read are the Supplicatory Canons to the Saviour and the Mother of God, and the Canon to the Guardian Angel (in that order), and either the Akathist to the Saviour or to the Mother of God. Those who desire to carry out this evening rule of prayer daily receive great spiritual benefit from doing so.

CONCERNING THE JESUS PRAYER

In the First Epistle to the Thessalonians the Apostle Paul says: *Pray without ceasing.* How, then, is one to pray unceasingly? By often repeating the Jesus Prayer: "Lord Jesus Christ, Son of God, have mercy on me." If one becomes accustomed to this appeal, great consolation and the need to continually make this petition will be felt within, and it will be carried on, as if of itself, within one.

Although in the beginning the enemy of the human race will offer hindrances to this, by causing great weariness, indolence, boredom, and over-powering sleep, having withstood all these with the help of God, one will receive peace of soul, spiritual joy, a benevolent disposition towards people, tranquility of thought, and gratitude toward God.

In the very name of Jesus Christ a great and graceful power is inherent.

Many holy and righteous people advise how one can often, almost without interruption, perform the Jesus Prayer.

Saint John Chrysostom says: "It is necessary for everyone, whether eating, drinking, sitting, serving, travelling, or doing anything, to unceasingly cry: 'Lord Jesus Christ, Son of

God, have mercy on me,' that the name of the Lord Jesus Christ, descending into the depths of the heart, may subdue the pernicious serpent, and save and quicken the soul.

Saint Seraphim of Sarov: "Lord Jesus Christ, Son of God, have mercy on me a sinner": let all thine attention and training be in this. Walking, sitting, doing, and standing in church before the divine service, coming in and going out, keep this unceasingly on thy lips and in thy heart. In calling in this manner on the name of God thou wilt find peace, thou wilt attain to purity of spirit and body, and the Holy Spirit, the Origin of all good things, will dwell in thee, and He will guide thee unto holiness, unto all piety and purity."

Bishop Theophanes the Recluse: "In order to more conveniently become accustomed to the remembrance of God, for this the fervent Christian has a special means, namely, to repeat unceasingly a brief prayer of two or three words. Most often this is: 'Lord, have mercy!' or 'Lord Jesus Christ, have mercy on me a sinner.' If you have not yet heard of this, then hear it now, and if you have not done it, then begin to do it from this time.

"Those who have truly decided to serve the

Lord God must train themselves in the remembrance of God and in unceasing prayer to Jesus Christ, saying mentally: 'Lord Jesus Christ, Son of God, have mercy on me a sinner.'

"Through such practice, by guarding oneself from distraction and by the preservation of the peace of one's conscience, it is possible to draw near to God and to be united with Him. For, according to the words of Saint Isaac the Syrian, 'Without unceasing prayer we cannot draw near to God' (St. Seraphim of Sarov)."

Saint John of Kronstadt likewise frequently counselled the doing of the Jesus Prayer.